Learn VueJs
in
7 Days

by
Dr. Vishal Jain
Nirmal Hota
Tadit Dash

Distributors:

BPB PUBLICATIONS
20, Ansari Road, Darya Ganj
New Delhi-110002
Ph: 23254990/23254991

DECCAN AGENCIES
4-3-329, Bank Street,
Hyderabad-500195
Ph: 24756967/24756400

MICRO MEDIA
Shop No. 5, Mahendra Chambers,
150 DN Rd. Next to Capital Cinema,
V.T. (C.S.T.) Station, MUMBAI-400 001
Ph: 22078296/22078297

BPB BOOK CENTRE
376 Old Lajpat Rai Market,
Delhi-110006
Ph: 23861747

Published by Manish Jain for BPB Publications, 20 Ansari Road, Darya Ganj, New Delhi-110002 and Printed by him at Repro India Ltd, Mumbai

About the Authors

Dr. Vishal Jain

He is currently working as Associate Professor with Bharati Vidyapeeth's Institute of Computer Applications and Management (BVICAM), New Delhi Affiliated to GGSIPU and Accredited by AICTE, since July, 2017 to till date. Dr. Vishal Jain has completed Ph.D (Computer Science and Engineering) from Lingaya's University, Faridabad, Haryana, M.Tech (Computer Science and Engineering) from University School of Information Technology (USIT), Guru Gobind Singh Indraprastha University, MBA (HR) from Shobhit University, Meerut, MCA from Sikkim Manipal University, Sikkim. In additional qualification he has obtained DOEACC 'A' Level and DOEACC 'O' Level, Post Graduate Diploma in Computer Software Training from A.M Informatics, Advance Diploma in Computer Software Training from ET&T, Delhi, Diploma in Business Management from All India Institute of Management Studies, Chennai, Diploma in Programming from Oxford Computer Education, Delhi, Microsoft Certified Professional Cleared Two Modules 070-210, 070-215 (MCP) and Cisco Certified Network Administrator (CCNA). He has received Young Active Member award for the year 2012 – 13 from Computer Society of India. Dr. Vishal Jain has worked as a Delhi State Students' Coordinator, Delhi Chapter, Computer Society of India (2014 – 2016). His research area includes Semantic Web, Ontology Engineering, Cloud Computing, Big Data Analytics and Adhoc Networks.

His Linkedin:
linkedin.com/in/vishaljain83

His Website
• vishaljain.webs.com

Nirmal Hota

He is a software developer and mentor. He loves to learn and work in different technologies. He has worked in various Microsoft Technologies such as C#, VB, ASP.net, Dynamics CRM, Commerce server and so on. Also worth mentioning his expertise in open source and mobile application technologies like Ruby on Rails, Phonegap, Titanium, Xamarin and so on. He loves to explore different Javascript based platforms including Angular, React and Vue.

He is also a Microsoft Certified Technology Specialist (MCTS) in Asp.Net and Dynamics CRM. In addition to that, he has also a Titanium Certified Application Developer(TCAD) and an Agile Scrum Master too.

Apart from developing software, he spends his time in tech community activities, blogging and creating screencast videos also. For his tech blogging activities and writing skills DZone has also recognised him as a Most Valuable Blogger. Utkal Techies Forum (UTF) and TechBhubaneswar are among two leading technical community in Odisha, India. In those communities, Nirmal is very much involved as a core group member. He also does a lot of tech speaking in various technologies in various conferences, schools, colleges and universities within India and abroad. India mentor has also featured him on their website to recognise his activity towards mentoring the community.

His Linkedin:
linkedin.com/in/nirmalhota

His Websites
- mindfiresolutions.com
- nirmalhota.com

Tadit Dash

He is a software engineer by profession. As a software engineer, he usually works for eight to nine hours daily. Besides his daily work, he contributes to both online and offline communities. He co-founded the first Technical Community in his state named Utkal Techies Forum Odisha, which is devoted to spreading awareness of the newest trends in technology among techies.

He writes articles and blogs, and creates demos and videos for fellow programmers. Answering questions on online forums and social channels is the activity he enjoys the most.

Due to his exceptional contribution to the technical community, Microsoft has awarded him with the Microsoft Most Valuable Professional accolade from 2014 till 2018. CodeProject has awarded him the CodeProject MVP accolade (the first from Odisha and three times in a row for the years 2014, 2015, and 2016). For his constant mentorship, IndiaMentor featured him as a Young Mentor on their site.

He was recognized by DZone and awarded the Most Valuable Blogger accolade.

Motivating students in his sessions is something he is popular for. He is a regular technical and motivational speaker. He has spoken in many local events organized by different communities. He was a featured speaker in DevTechDay Nepal.

The following two books he co-authored got Bestseller ranks on Amazon and were featured on Book Authority's "Best ASP.NET Books of All Time".

- Dependency Injection in .NET Core 2.0
- Building RESTful Web services using .NET Core

You can reach him on Facebook, Twitter and Instagram at @taditdash.

His Linkedin:

linkedin.com/in/taditdash

His Websites

- taditdash.wordpress.com

Acknowledgements

Nirmal Hota

This book is a reality today because of the blessing and encouragement of my parents (Mr. Niranjan Hota and Mrs. Bishnupriya Hota). Spending time to write a book after a full day of office work was a big challenge and my family around me kept me motivated continuously to achieve the same.

I am very much thankful to my Wife (Subhshree Hota), my brother (Nikhil Hota), my sisters (Silu and Milu) , my brother in laws (Dilip and Shakti) and loving kids (Gagu, Tatu and Kitu) for the love and support.

My heartiest thanks and respect to Mr. Santanu Mohapatra, my guru, who has enlightened the spark of knowledge in me. I am also thankful to Mr. Gaurav Aroraa, the renowned author and mentor, for his uncountable support and love towards me. Also my thanks and respect to Dr. Vishal Jain, the co-author of this book for his guidance during this period.

Thank you Mr Tadit Dash, co-author, colleague and my little bro, for pulling up the best out of me. I would also like to thank Suvendu Sekhar Giri, Surya Narayan Barik, Pravasini Sahu, Suraj Sahu, Ramesh Barik, Sourav Nanda, and UTF for helping me to explore myself.

Thank you very much to my colleagues, Mr. Kiran Kumar Singh and Debendra Nandi for teaching me various approaches to deal with challenges. Finally a huge thanks to BPB publications for making all these into reality.

Tadit Dash

I would like to dedicate this book to my grand father late *Ganeswar Tripathy*.

My grandmother *Santipriya Tripathy*, father *Dr. Gobinda Chandra Dash*, mother *Mrs. Sasmita Tripathy* and brother *Tworit Dash* made sure that I am high on energy (with healthy food) and confidence all the time during the writing. My uncles *Mr. Anil Tripathy, Mr. Aswin Tripathy* and *Mr. Amiya Tripathy* always guide me to shape the approach to my new challenges. *Mrs. Sujata Tripathy*, who takes care of me like my mother and *Mr. Debendra Rath*, my uncle never miss any opportunity to discuss ideas to strengthen my thoughts so that I deliver the best.

My guide, mentor *Mr. Gaurav Kumar Arora* (who is a renowned author) encouraged me to take up the project and constantly motivated throughout the preparation. I am so grateful to the BPB team for their constant inputs to make the project beautiful. Thanks to *Mr. Nirmal Hota* (co-author of this book), who is like my big brother, for his consistent effort in throwing me out of my comfort zone while patting my back. *Miss. Prakreeti Prasanna*, as a well wisher and best friend, always adds a x-factor to my activities. All my friends, family members, colleagues and Google, of course, are the ingredients for the success of this book. Special thanks to my community members of *"Utkal Techies Forum"* for waiting to hear the surprise.

Last, but not least, *Mrs. Jayashree Satapathy*, who being the best part of life has taken every care to make my writing schedule smooth.

Preface

Coming from professional and educational background, we as authors decided to come up with a reasonable book to cater the quest for knowledge regarding JavaScript frameworks that prevails over the industry in the current era.

When we see businesses adhere to a particular framework or technology for the projects, the decision largely depends upon the developers or architects to come up with the actual implementation procedure. This book acts as a handy tool to learn the simplicity of VueJs so that the stakeholders would take appropriate measures when selecting it over other frameworks in competition.

You might find different books in the market on the same topic, however, our book particularly focuses on the step by step approach to learn the framework with proper illustrations. Most importantly, whys and hows are intelligently responded for the concepts. If you follow the book chapter by chapter, after 7 days, you would definitely make yourself comfortable in VueJs without any hassels.

While designing the book, we have taken proper care to present the concepts from the basics of VueJs. However, we assume that you at least have a basic understanding of how web development is done using HTML, JavaScript and CSS. We recommend this for students as well as working professionals who want to dive into VueJs. For students, it would help adding the skill to their resume, while for professionals, it would help them kick start and take better decisions for the existing and new projects they work on.

From the book, you can expect a detailed step by step learning path in each chapter with proper example codes. The explanations are well accompanied by screenshots so that you can quickly refer the output produced. In case of issues, don't hesitate to send us your queries.

Errata

We take immense pride in our work at BPB Publications and follow best practices to ensure the accuracy of our content to provide with an indulging reading experience to our subscribers. Our readers are our mirrors, and we use their inputs to reflect and improve upon human errors if any, occurred during the publishing processes involved. To let us maintain the quality and help us reach out to any readers who might be having difficulties due to any unforeseen errors, please write to us at :

errata@bpbonline.com

Your support, suggestions and feedbacks are highly appreciated by the BPB Publications' Family.

Table of Contents

Day 1
Introduction

In this chapter, we will go through an introduction of VueJS. We will also go through the Vue ecosystem to setup the environment. We will also cover a brief description on the installation process, devtools and vue CLI for project scaffolding, and so on in this chapter.

As we know, JavaScript is a scripting language being interpreted by the browser, with the help of embedded JavaScript engines such as V8, Rhino, and so on. V8 is the most widely used JS engine in the modern web browsers. JavaScript plays a vital role in the world of web development by executing the user request in the client end and reducing the client-server request response roundtrip, which enhances the user experience and performance.

Vue is a UI based framework built on top of JavaScript. It works on the UI layer of the web applications.

Before I start with VueJS

Since it is a JavaScript based framework, it mainly operates on the UI layer, it requires for the developers to know the basics of JavaScript, HTML, and CSS so that the user can implement VueJS in the project to see it in action.

In this book, we will keep using the VueJS along with the normal JavaScript.

VueJS

VueJS is an open source progressive JavaScript framework. It is originally invented by Evan You, one of the ex-Google employee. He has worked in MeteroJS project as well. Although graduated from Arts, he is in touch with development. He got a chance to work with Angular during his Google days. He then started working in his own project and the first VueJS version was pushed to Git in February 2014, which arguably seems to as an improvement over Angular.

VueJS has some key characteristics which make it popular and adoptable.

Light weight

It is light weight JavaScript library which comes into action, as soon as it's added to the project. It mainly follows a ViewModel pattern to communicate with the view layer. The view layer is mainly designed with HTML and CSS.

Progressive

As mentioned earlier, it basically works on the View layer in the UI. It is implemented as an additional markup to the HTML UI by binding the template model with data model.

Virtual DOM

DOM is the abbreviation for Document Object Model. The HTML DOM in the browser we see, has a tree like structure. In order to make changes in the UI in the browser, we need to make changes to the DOM element by finding that from the DOM tree. Mostly we use *document.getElementById* to find the element. This is a memory expensive process which makes the page perform slower.

Virtual DOM is a technique to bind the DOM tree to the JavaScript object tree. The JavaScript object tree is not the actual DOM, it is a virtual representation of the HTML DOM on UI. So, any changes to any of the JavaScript object attribute node which binds with a DOM element will get reflected on screen UI. This would NOT be a memory expensive way. Implementation of Virtual DOM in Vue, based on **snabbdom (https://github.com/snabbdom/snabbdom)**.

HTML based template

Template helps in creating re-usable UI components. Vue object allows defining the templates by using the HTML code within the object itself, which helps in creating the reusable components as well as it adds advancement to the existing HTML.

Reactive view components

Vue supports the two-way binding technique. The data model is bind to the template model which reflects on UI, when changes made to the data in the data model and vice versa.

Single Page Application

Single page applications (SPA) are the kind of web application which basically renders and re-renders by dynamically writing contents in the same page than loading multiple pages for the contents depending upon the user actions. Vue can be used to develop SPA. It can also be used in multi-page applications as well.

Let's setup VueJs

We need to setup the Vue now, in order to use it in our project. So, before we proceed and install it in the project, let's first check the number of ways we can add VueJS to our project.

Download and reference method

As mentioned earlier, Vue is a lightweight JS library. This library can be directly downloaded and added to the project, by using the **<script/>** tag. It has two versions available, for download and to be used in the page.

Development version: https://vuejs.org/js/vue.js

It is advisable to use this version during the development phase. This is a non-minified version with relevant debug and warning message, which helps the developer during development.

Production Version: https://vuejs.org/js/vue.min.js

The production version is the gzipped minified version of the library with reduced size of approximately 31KB. It suppresses the debug and warning messages, which won't be used in the production anyway.

The JS library can be downloaded/saved from the above location to be used in the project. So that it will also be available offline during development.

Although this can be referenced directly as an online link but it would be slower. If intended to refer online, it is advisable to use the CDN method, which will be explained now.

Reference from CDN

CDN reference is same as the download method. The basic difference is, in the direct download method, it is advisable to download the JS and use in the **<script/>** tag. But in the CDN, it will directly be referenced from the CDN in the project. It will be faster to get loaded into the page, although referenced from online.

<script src="https://cdn.jsdelivr.net/npm/vue@2.5.17/dist/vue.js" />

It is also advisable to use the non-minified version during development, which helps in debugging. CDN reference method helps the user to reference the required version of Vue, as shown in the above code example. We have referenced the version 2.5.17 of the Vue library. The version must be manually updated to point to the correct one.

The other available Vue versions can be browsed from the NPM package, as shown in the image below. Version can be changed from the version dropdown, to view the package contents.

Fig 1.1: Vuejs CDN file structure

Other CDN services like unpkg and cdnjs can be referenced as well.

unpkg **<script src="https://unpkg.com/vue@2.5.17/dist/vue.js" />**

cdnjs **<script src="https://cdnjs.cloudflare.com/ajax/libs/vue/2.5.17/vue.js" />**

While deploying to the production, **vue.js** needs to be changed as **vue.min.js**.

Using NPM

*Node Package Manager (NPM) is the default package manager from NodeJS. Details about NPM is beyond the scope of this book. Please make sure, NodeJS and NPM is already installed in your machine. You can setup NPM from. To know the NodeJS and NPM version, execute **node -v** and **npm -v** in the command line respectively.*

Vue can also be installed using NPM from the command line. Once installed using NPM, Vue needs to be imported into the project. Run the following command to install Vue using NPM method to install the latest build.

$ npm install vue

Before running the preceding command, make sure that NPM must be installed in your machine. The above installed command creates the folder structure and installs the node modules for the latest version of Vue.

Fig 1.2: NPM folder structure for Vue after the project creation

The preceding image represents the folder structure of the installed VueJS NPM package. Now, in order to use the Vue in our project, we need to add the vue.js path to our script tag. Following is the sample code, which shows how it would look like.

```
<!DOCTYPE html >
<html>
    <head>
        <script src="../node_modules/vue/dist/vue.js"></
script>
    </head>
    <body>
        <div id="hello_msg">
```

```
        {{ hello_msg }}
    </div>
    <script>
        var v1 = new Vue({
            el: "#hello_msg",
            data: {
                hello_msg: "Hello Readers"
            }
        });
    </script>
</body>
</html>
```

This code is just to show, how we can use the Vue.JS library after NPM install. The **bold** line in the code indicates the Vue reference. We will traverse through the code in later topics. The vue.js file referenced here is the development version of the vue, so that developer can get the warning and debug messages during the development. But before pushing this to the production, we need to change the reference to vue.min.js.

Let's put Vue into action

We will start putting Vue in HTML page and see the effect in browser. We will use the CDN links to include VueJS into the page.

Let's create a document and name it as **index.html.** In the **index. html,** we will add the following code to see Vue in action.

```
<!DOCTYPE html >
<html>
    <head>
            <script src="https://cdn.jsdelivr.net/npm/
vue@2.5.17/dist/vue.js"></script>
    </head>
    <body>
            <div id="hello_msg">
                {{ hello_msg }}
            </div>
```

```
<script>
    var v1 = new Vue({
        el: "#hello_msg",
        data: {
            hello_msg: "Hello Readers"
        }
    });
</script>
</body>
</html>
```

Now, let's view the **index.html** file in the browser.

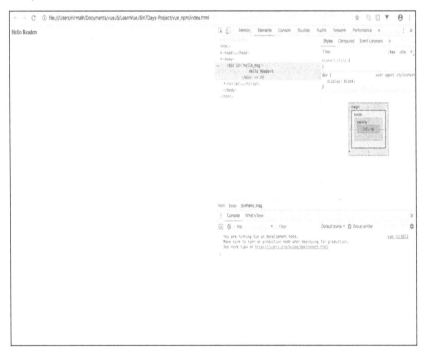

Fig 1.3: Showing Index.html in the web browser

As we can see in the browser through the inspection tool in the left, our message is getting displayed inside the div.

Let's analyze the index.html code

Add VueJS reference

The **<script>** tag in the **<head>** section contains the link to VueJS. While this gets rendered in the browser, it will pull the VueJS library from the mentioned CDN and includes the same to our page. Thus, the VueJS library is available to the page and we would be able to create the Vue object to work on the DOM elements.

Create Vue object

Now come to the next **<script>** tag that is present inside the **<body>**. In this section, we are initializing the Vue object for the page. Now, Vue object needs to operate on an HTML DOM element.

Specify the DOM element for Vue object

In the Vue object, **el** is the element attribute. It accepts the HTML element on which Vue object will operate. Since we are using **hello_ msg** as ID of the **<div>** element, we have prepended the # selector while specifying the element in the **el** attribute to access the DOM element.

We can also use the . selector to specify as .hello_msg in the el attribute of Vue object, if css class is used instead of id.

Data attribute of Vue object

Let's look at the data attribute of the Vue object. It contains the data to be rendered on the screen. In our example above, **hello_msg** is the data variable, which holds the message to be displayed on the screen. So, we have assigned a hard-coded text i.e. **Hello Readers**, to our data variable.

Display the data attribute on screen

Inside the **<div>** tag, we are now ready to render the message in the browser. We have used the mustache representation to show the data attribute of Vue object on the screen. In this example, {{ **hello_msg**

}} looks for the **hello_msg** variable in the data attribute of the Vue object. As soon as it finds the variable in there, it renders its value on the screen.

We can have multiple data variables in the data attribute of Vue object, which we will anyway cover in the rest part of the book. We can have multiple Vue objects in a single page as well in the **<script>** sections.

Now, save this **index.html** page and try viewing the same in any browser. You will see the output, as string in the browser rendering the **Hello Readers** string.

> *Incase, you are wondering, can we use CSS? Can we use a separate JS file to define the Vue object? For your info, the answer is YES for all these questions. We can have CSS styling applied to HTML as a normal way, without any extra steps.*

Vue Devtools

Vue devtools, as the name suggests, it is the tool for the developers in order to debug the rendering outputs in the runtime. It allows the user to debug the Vue object at runtime. We can browse to see the Root Vue object, its attributes, methods and events along with the other dependent object in a tree like presentation.

Devtools can be added to browsers like Chrome, Fireforx etc. as an extension to debug the Vue application.

As a browser extension, it renders vue object view in the inspection window of the bowser.

The following image points to the Vue object we have created in our earlier example to display the **hello_msg** string on screen.

The **<Root>** points to the Vue object. On selecting the **<Root>**, it displays the attributes of the object in the right-side pane. The data attribute shows the **hello_msg** variable and its content. We can also edit the value of the **hello_msg** variable here to see the effect on screen immediately.

Fig 1.4: *vue devtools browsing the Vue object in the DOM*

Install the dev tools in Chrome

- Open the Chrome browser
- Go to the **Three Dot Menu Icon | More Tools | Extensions page**
- Search for Vue.js devtools
- Click on install to install the extension

Upon successful installation, it will be shown in the browser as an extension. It works fine with pages using Vue object.

If you want to access the Vue.JS devtools in file:// protocol then you need to enable the **Allow access to file URLs** option in the Vue.JS devtools extension settings.

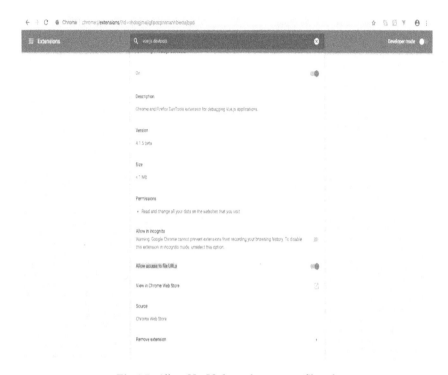

Fig 1.5: *Allow VueJS devtools to access file urls*

Install the dev tools in Firefox

- Open the Firefox browser
- Go to the **Three Bar Menu Icon | Add-ons page**
- Click on **Extensions** option
- Search for Vue.js devtools
- Click on **Install** to install the add on

Now, dev tools are available for debugging the Vue object.

If the page is using production/minified version of VueJS, then the Vue pane wont show up.

I don't use Chrome and Firefox. Can I also debug?

Yes, the good news is, you can also debug the Vue application. VueJS offers the standalone electron app **(https://github.com/vuejs/**

vue-devtools/blob/master/shells/electron/README.md) helps to setup the **vuejs-remote-devtools** to allow the developers to debug the application in any environment. It can work with Safari, Mobile Browsers, IE, and so on.

Vue CLI

Vue **Command Line Interface (CLI)** is the command line interface to create, run and build the vue application. It is the way to setup a project rapidly under a single command. Vue CLI scaffold the vue project when we try to create a new one by adding all the plugins and references automatically as it has been chosen.

Setup the Vue CLI

In order to setup the Vue CLI, we will use the **npm**.

$ npm install -g @vue/cli

The above command installs the Vue CLI in global scope. So that we can invoke the commands from the command line directly, without any project or folder dependency. You can use **sudo**, if you are not logged in as a root user in Mac/Linux.

Create project

After the successful installation, we can run the following command to rapidly create our Vue app project. It will automatically create the project by adding the required plugins and references to it.

$ vue create hello-vue

It will start the process of creating a new project named as **hello-vue**. Upon executing the create command, Vue CLI offer two options to us, to proceed and create the project.

- Proceed with default option with Babel and ESLint
- Proceed by choosing manually

Let's create with default option

```
Vue CLI v3.0.4
? Please pick a preset:
> default (babel, eslint)
  Manually select features
```

Fig 1.6: Creating Vue project with default options

> ***Babel** is an open source JavaScript compiler. It converts the edged JavaScript to plain old JavaScript code for backward compatibility. So that the older browsers can also understand it. As we keep writing the JavaScript in Vue, Babel will be used to compile the same as needed for the browsers to understand.*
>
> ***ESLint** is a linting tool to validate the patterns and styles of the JavaScript before executing them. It would be very helpful for the developers to know the issues and mistakes with the syntax and rules with executing the JavaScript.*

Upon hitting *Enter*, it will start creating the new project and adds all the hooks and plugin into the project.

As shown in the image below, it has already created the project by adding the desired hooks, plugins, and so on.

```
setting up Git hooks
done

added 1350 packages from 771 contributors and audited 13877 packages in 47.831s
found   vulnerabilities

  Invoking generators...
  Installing additional dependencies...

added 3 packages from 1 contributor and audited 13881 packages in 16.2s
found   vulnerabilities

  Running completion hooks...

  Generating README.md...

  Successfully created project hello-vue.
  Get started with the following commands:

  $ cd hello-vue
  $ npm run serve
```

Fig 1.7: Console output after the Vue project gets created

Let's create with manual option

Manual option allows us to create the Vue project by selecting the plugins and hooks manually as needed.

$ vue create hello-vue-again

After we run the create command, it will again take us to the same screen and ask to choose the options to create the project. We will hit the down arrow key to select the **Manually select features** option and hit enter.

```
Vue CLI v3.0.4
? Please pick a preset: Manually select features
? Check the features needed for your project: (Press <space> to select, <a> to toggle all, <i> to invert selection)
>o Babel
 o TypeScript
 o Progressive Web App (PWA) Support
 o Router
 o Vuex
 o CSS Pre-processors
 ● Linter / Formatter
 o Unit Testing
 o E2E Testing
```

Fig 1.8: Creating vue project by choosing the options manually

As shown in the image, the Babel and Linter are selected by default. We can select other options by keeping the default ones as well. We are free to choose the features as needed, by hitting the **<space>** bar.

Once the selection of features are done, we can hit enter to proceed with the options to create the project. It keeps asking the features to select as per the previous option selection.

```
Vue CLI v3.0.4
? Please pick a preset: Manually select features
? Check the features needed for your project: Babel, Linter
? Pick a linter / formatter config: Basic
? Pick additional lint features: Lint on save
? Where do you prefer placing config for Babel, PostCSS, ESLint, etc.? In dedicated config files
? Save this as a preset for future projects? (y/N)
```

*Fig 1.9: Console displaying and accepting the manual
options while creating VueJS Project*

As stated in the image, I have selected all the default ones in the list. You might have some different options/queries based on your previous selection. After the last query chosen, it proceeds to create project.

The currently chosen/entered options can be saved under a user specified name to reuse the same. **Preset** is a configuration file to store those chosen customized options. It stores the options in a key-value pair format in **.vuerc** file in the user's home directory under a user specified format.

Following is the **.vuerc** file that stored the above selected options. I have stored in the name of **hello-vue-again**.

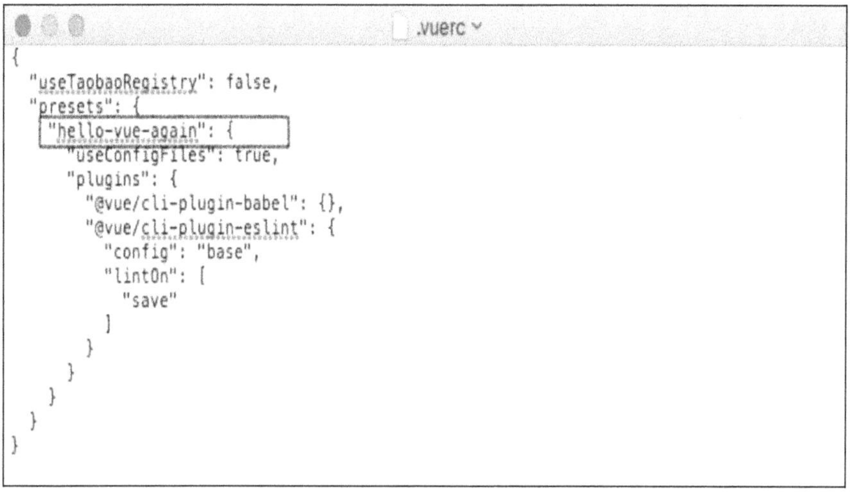

```
                                        .vuerc ⌄
{
  "useTaobaoRegistry": false,
  "presets": {
    "hello-vue-again": {
      "useConfigFiles": true,
      "plugins": {
        "@vue/cli-plugin-babel": {},
        "@vue/cli-plugin-eslint": {
          "config": "base",
          "lintOn": [
            "save"
          ]
        }
      }
    }
  }
}
```

Fig 1.10: .vuerc file content

How it looks like in the runtime?

Now, project is ready to run with the minimal plugins with it. We should see the default pages now in the browser.

We can now, navigate to the newly created project folder i.e. **Hello-vue** and run the **serve** command to see the project in browser.

$ cd hello-vue

$ npm run serve

Serve command here, initialize and runs the development server. Builds links and refers the necessary modules and plugins. Finally exposes the project to 8080 port for viewing.

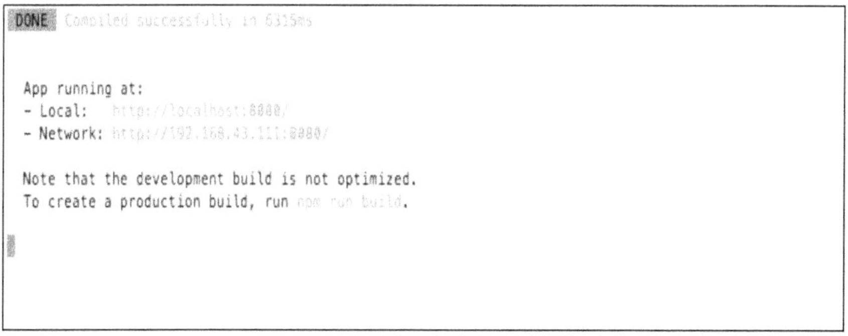

```
DONE  Compiled successfully in 6315ms


App running at:
- Local:   http://localhost:8080/
- Network: http://192.168.43.111:8080/

Note that the development build is not optimized.
To create a production build, run npm run build.
```

Fig 1.11: Console output after the successful server
start to view the project in web browser

As shown in the preceding image, the output can be browsed from the 8080 port from the local browser. Also, the same can be accessed by the computers in the same LAN with the local IP of the computer in which the development server is running.

Fig 1.12: VueJS HelloWorld project starts with default UI in web browser

Analyse the project

Let's analyse the project file tree automatically setup by CLI. We will analyse the **hello-vue** project, which we have created earlier.

Fig 1.13: Hello-vue project file structure

babel.config.js: It stores the babel configuration.

node_modules: This folder contains the relevant node modules and plugins needed for the project. It depends upon the user selection of features while creating the project.

package.json: Packge.json file stores the modules, services, dependencies, and so on. used in the project along with the project information.

```json
{
  "name": "hello-vue",
  "version": "0.1.0",
  "private": true,
  "scripts": {
    "serve": "vue-cli-service serve",
    "build": "vue-cli-service build",
    "lint": "vue-cli-service lint"
  },
  "dependencies": {
    "vue": "^2.5.17"
  },
  "devDependencies": {
    "@vue/cli-plugin-babel": "^3.0.4",
    "@vue/cli-plugin-eslint": "^3.0.4",
    "@vue/cli-service": "^3.0.4",
    "vue-template-compiler": "^2.5.17"
  },
  "eslintConfig": {
    "root": true,
    "env": {
      "node": true
    },
    "extends": [
      "plugin:vue/essential",
      "eslint:recommended"
    ],
    "rules": {},
    "parserOptions": {
      "parser": "babel-eslint"
    }
  },
  "postcss": {
    "plugins": {
      "autoprefixer": {}
    }
  },
  "browserslist": [
    "> 1%",
    "last 2 versions",
    "not ie <= 8"
  ]
}
```

Fig 1.14: package.json file content

package-lock.json: It contains mostly the same information as **package.json**, but additionally locks down the version of the package used in the project. So that while updating, the package won't make the app malfunctioning. It will point to the locked version only, unless changed explicitly.

```
{
  "name": "hello-vue",
  "version": "0.1.0",
  "lockfileVersion": 1,
  "requires": true,
  "dependencies": {
    "@babel/code-frame": {
      "version": "7.0.0-beta.47",
      "resolved": "https://registry.npmjs.org/@babel/code-frame/-/code-frame-7.0.0-beta.47.tgz",
      "integrity": "sha512-W7IeG4MoVf4oUvWfHUx9VG9if3E0x5UDf1urrnNYtC2ow1dz2ptvQ6YsJfyVXDuPTFXz66jkHhzMW7a5Eld7T
      "dev": true,
      "requires": {
        "@babel/highlight": "7.0.0-beta.47"
      }
    },
    "@babel/core": {
      "version": "7.0.0-beta.47",
      "resolved": "https://registry.npmjs.org/@babel/core/-/core-7.0.0-beta.47.tgz",
      "integrity": "sha512-7EIuAX0UVnCgZ0E9tz9rfK8gd+aovwMA9bul+dnkmBQYLrJdas2EHMUSmaK67i1cyZpvgVvXhHtXJxC7wo3rl
      "dev": true,
      "requires": {
        "@babel/code-frame": "7.0.0-beta.47",
        "@babel/generator": "7.0.0-beta.47",
        "@babel/helpers": "7.0.0-beta.47",
        "@babel/template": "7.0.0-beta.47",
        "@babel/traverse": "7.0.0-beta.47",
        "@babel/types": "7.0.0-beta.47",
        "babylon": "7.0.0-beta.47",
        "convert-source-map": "^1.1.0",
        "debug": "^3.1.0",
        "json5": "^0.5.0",
        "lodash": "^4.17.5",
        "micromatch": "^2.3.11",
        "resolve": "^1.3.2",
        "semver": "^5.4.1",
        "source-map": "^0.5.0"
      }
    },
```

Fg 1.15: package-lock.json

public: Public folder normally contains the resources, which need not to be compile multiple times during page view. Such as images, **index.html** page, and so on.

src: It is the source folder that contains the source code for the project.

App.vue: Contains the html template code to be rendered inside the **index.html**.

assets: All the local assets such as images, css and so on.

components: This folder contains the vue components.

main.js: Used to initialize the vue object in the desired DOM.

How this works

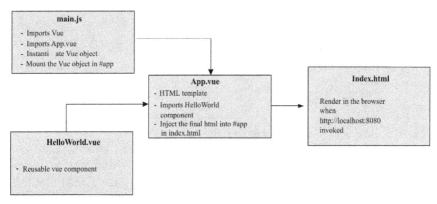

It first invokes the **main.js**. This file contains the initial import of the vue module and initializes the vue object.

```
import Vue from 'vue'
import App from './App.vue'

Vue.config.productionTip = false

new Vue({
  render: h => h(App)
}).$mount('#app')
```

Fig 1.16: main.js content in the hello-vue project

It is importing the vue from the **node_modules**. Since the execution starts from **main.js**, it will first import the **vue** module and **App.vue** template into the project. After the import, it creates the vue object and mount the same in the #**app** DOM element.

Find # app DOM

It is time to locate the #app DOM element, so that the above vue object gets initialized with that.

```html
<!DOCTYPE html>
<html lang="en">
  <head>
    <meta charset="utf-8">
    <meta http-equiv="X-UA-Compatible" content="IE=edge">
    <meta name="viewport" content="width=device-width,initial-scale=1.0">
    <link rel="icon" href="<%= BASE_URL %>favicon.ico">
    <title>hello-vue</title>
  </head>
  <body>
    <noscript>
      <strong>We're sorry but hello-vue doesn't work properly without JavaScript enabled. Please enable it to continue.</strong>
    </noscript>
    <div id="app"></div>
    <!-- built files will be auto injected -->
  </body>
</html>
```

Fig 1.17: Index.html

In the above **index.html** code, we can see the **<div id="app"></div>.**
Now, the vue object in **main.js** will be created on this DOM element
and **app.vue** template gets injected into this **<div>** element.

Review App.vue template

```html
<template>
  <div id="app">
    <img alt="Vue logo" src="./assets/logo.png">
    <HelloWorld msg="Welcome to Your Vue.js App"/>
  </div>
</template>

<script>
import HelloWorld from './components/HelloWorld.vue'

export default {
  name: 'app',
  components: {
    HelloWorld
  }
}
</script>

<style>
#app {
  font-family: 'Avenir', Helvetica, Arial, sans-serif;
  -webkit-font-smoothing: antialiased;
  -moz-osx-font-smoothing: grayscale;
  text-align: center;
  color: #2c3e50;
  margin-top: 60px;
}
</style>
```

Fig 1.18: HelloWorld.vue

As in this code, it imports the **HelloWorld.vue** component to be rendered inside this template. That means, the **HelloWorld.vue** component gets rendered in the **App.Vue** template and the template will be rendered inside the **index.html.** So, that we get the full page rendered in the browser.

Deployment

It is all done with the prototyping, debugging, and evaluating. Now, it's the time to setup the app in a server, so that we can put the app in use.

$ cd hello-vue

$ npm run build

The **build** command creates the outputs for the deployment into the server. Upon successful running of the command, it generates a **dist** folder with all the required files to be deployed.

Behind the scene, it compiles and prepares the static resources to be deployed in the **dist** folder. These static contents of the **dist** folder can be deployed to the server.

VueJS UI

We have just completed the project with Vue CLI. The same can be done using a **Graphical User Interface (GUI).**

$ vue ui

It runs the GUI in 8080 port and allow the user to:

- Create a new vue project
- Import an existing project
- Serve the project to review and validate the prototype
- Build the project for deployment
- Add remove plugins and dependencies
- Add/edit configuration

Fig 1.19: Graphical User Interface (GUI) to create Vue project

The **Projects** tab will display the list of projects created and imported in it. We can remove the projects and open the project in an editor from this tab.

🔍 **summary**

In this chapter we have covered a brief introduction to Vue and its object creation mechanism, setting up of the Vue eco-system, Vue CLI to scaffold a vue project along with the Vue UI to manage the projects.

In the next chapter, we will move forward with some close step towards the deep into the coding part. We will learn how really the DOM and Vue object binding works with different DOM elements. It will also cover the conditional statements and control flow used in Vue.

DAY 2
Rendering with HTML

In the previous chapter, we could able to run our first basic application using Vue.js. Moreover, we learned techniques to start coding, then debugging with Vue.js devtools and deploy the application using Vue UI tool.

Going forward, in this chapter, I will explain you how exactly Vue comes into the picture while rendering one html page. We will explore different useful syntaxes to work with Vue library in order to perform basic operations with data and event handlings.

Vue provides easy to use syntaxes to attach data to HTML elements. Mustaches syntax with Vue is a very basic, yet totally handy mechanism to quickly render data. When it comes to deal with different attributes of one HTML elements, Vue would back you up with interesting directives which is the heart of this chapter.

HTML Form elements are used to take user inputs and it's always necessary to make them responsive to data changes whether from user side or from the backend which can be easily managed by two way data binding provided by Vue. Obviously, we will discuss more on this in the chapter. Stay tuned. Moreover, we will see how we can attach simple click and change events with the HTML elements.

Following are the topics we will cover:

- Basic HTML structuring with Vue
- Condition and Loop structure
- Form elements and basic event handling

Basic HTML structuring with Vue

While introducing you to Vue in that previous chapter, you got to know about the structure by which we can include the Vue.js library and start working on the Vue object for the application.

Let's analyze again with a simple html page with Vue syntax.

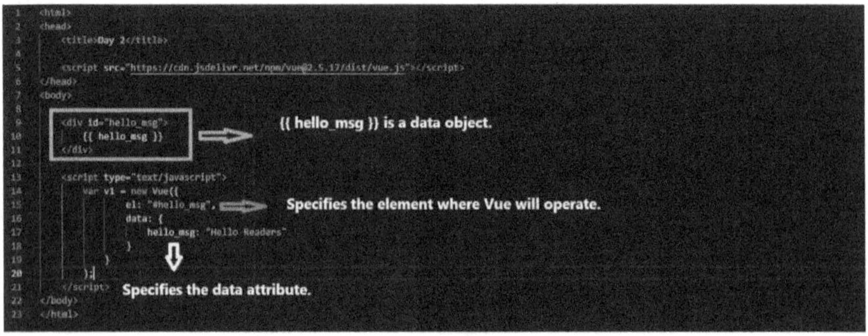

Fig 2.1: Simple HTML Page with Vue

Important things to note here are as follows :

- **The el attribute:** the el attribute inside the Vue object defines the element of DOM where Vue will start it's operation. Here we have #**hello_msg**. That means the element having **hello_ msg** as the id will be considered.

- **The data attribute:** this attribute can hold multiple data variables. For instance, we have one variable **hello_msg,** which is assigned a value as **Hello Readers**.

- **The DOM element:** this is the actual element on the page where Vue starts the operation. In our case, there is a div element, which is attached to the Vue object by the el attribute.

- **The binding {{ hello_msg }}:** is the one, who is actually responsible to render the data onto the screen.

Text Binding

The above mentioned binding is called *Text* binding and the double curly braces used, is called *Mustache* syntax.

Let's play with the data object and see whether the UI is responding to our updates or not.

```
<div id="hello_msg">
<button onclick="UpdateMessage('Hey dude, I am
changed!')">Update the Message</button>
      {{ hello_msg }}
</div>
```

Simple, I added one button and called a JavaScript function called as **Update Message**. Let's see what is inside this method.

```
function UpdateMessage(msg) {
    v1.hello_msg = msg;
}
```

Pretty clear, isn't it! assigning the value passed to this method to the data property **hello_msg** by taking help of the object **v1**. The **var v1** is the Vue object initialized on our html page. Refer the html screenshot in the last section.

After updating the code, run the file and click on the button. You will see something as follows :

Fig 2.2: Updating Data Property on Button Click

Notice that we did not write a single line of code to do anything to the UI. We changed the data property and it triggered an automatic update for the UI associated with it. This is where the property with Mustache syntax came into picture. Vue could be able to update the part, where it found that syntax.

Imagine, if you do this with jQuery. You have to get the div element and then you need to find the wrapping element of the actual message (which we don't have here). After that, you have to change the message by taking help of those elements. Of couse, Vue seems clean and easy. It not only simplified the task, but also made the code modularized by separating the data from UI.

Can you restrict the behavior of not updating the UI when property is changed? Yes, in some cases you might have a situation to do that and of course, that option is available. Let's see how.

```
<span v-once>{{ hello_msg }}</span>
```

We wrapped the message with a span and added one keyword v-once which is otherwise called as directive. Now, if you run the page, the message won't change with button click.

The v-once would restrict update of all the properties inside it. That means irrespective of how many data property or elements you have, if the parent element is having v-once, then all the UI inside is going to be rendered once and not going to change.

For example, consider the following mark up :

```
<div id="onlyOnce" v-once>
        <span>{{ hello_msg }}</span>

        <span>{{ dude_msg }}</span>
</div>
```

Here I have one div and two spans inside it with two data properties. However, I have marked the parent div with v-once. That means it will just print this data property values once. The point is v-once does not depend on a single property, it can restrict update for multiple properties.

Let's move to the next type of binding.

Raw HTML

When it comes to rendering HTML, Mustaches syntax is not going to help. It's going to render as plain text only. However, we have another binding to render HTML and that is through v-html directive.

Following is the syntax comparison:

```
<div>Html rendered as plain text (with Mustaches): <span>{{
rawHtmlTest }}</span></div>
```

```
<div>Html rendered as actual HTML (with v-html directive):
<span v-html="rawHtmlTest"></span></div>
```

When you run, we get the following output, provided, you supply the data property as:

rawHtmlTest: `"<div style='border:1px solid'>I am an HTML element with border!</div>"`

Fig 2.3: HTML Rendering

That means we wanted to render one div with a border. Mustaches could not be able to render, but v-html directive perfectly rendered our div.

Attributes

With Mustaches, you can't supply values to all HTML elements. Suppose, you have one textbox and you need to attach one Vue property to it. Unfortunately, we can't do with Mustaches. We need some other method.

For instance, an input field has a value attribute which is the content that it shows. That means, we need to somehow assign the data property to the value attribute of input, so that it displays the data. And here comes our v-bind directive. Let's see how we can do.

```
<input v-bind:value="hello_msg"/>
```

Output comes as follows:

We can bind Vue property to any attribute. Let' see how we can attach id.

```
<input v-bind:id="someId"/>
```

The image below shows the rendered HTML of the input on the browser. See how some **id** attribute is interpreted as **1234**, which is assigned inside the Vue object.

Fig 2.4: Binding Id Attribute

When you consider enable/disable like scenario, (that means a boolean value) you can do that like the following:

```
<input type="button" value="Hit Me"
    v-bind:disabled="isDisabled" />
```

If is **Disabled** is true, the button will be disabled. Let's see the output as well as the rendered HTML.

```
▼<div id="hello_msg">
    <input id="1234"> == $0
</div>
```

Fig 2.5: Disabled Attribute with Vue

See the button is in disable mode due to the disabled property added to the html rendered.

Interestingly, if the is **Disabled** value is false/null/undefined, the "disabled" attribute won't be added to the element at all. Let's do that and see what happens!

```
var v1 = new Vue({
        el: "#hello_msg",
        data: {
                //isDisabled: false
        }
    }
);
```

Let's comment out the property and then tried to running, refer the following screenshot from the web browser:

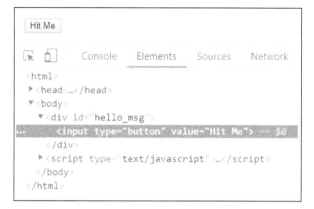

Fig 2.6: Disabled Attribute not Rendered

Notice that **disabled** attribute is not included and button is enabled. Moreover, you will get warning on the developer tool console window as follows:

```
▶ [Vue warn]: Property or method "isDisabled" is not defined on the vue.js:597
instance but referenced during render. Make sure that this property is
reactive, either in the data option, or for class-based components, by
initializing the property. See: https://vuejs.org/v2/guide/reactivity.html#Dec
laring-Reactive-Properties.

(found in <Root>)
```

Fig 2.7: Property is Disabled not defined error

This happened because we have commented the property inside the Vue object and it is clearly mentioned by Vue engine that the property is not defined.

JavaScript Expressions

JavaScript Expressions can be included with Vue to bring dynamicity. So, you can use the JavaScript syntaxes easily with Vue without any complex structure.

Let's take a look with some simple examples. If you add one data object count:3 to Vue object and write the following HTML on page, then the output will be as shown on the following screenshot:

Result Count: {{ count == 0 ? 'No results!': count + ' results!' }}

Output:

Fig 2.8: JavaScript Expression with Ternary Operator

You can use any valid JavaScript code inside the curly braces or v-bind as long as it is a single expression. Let me explain. Before that, refer another example.

Suppose we have a Vue data variable defined as follows:

vueMessage: "I am Vue! Love you."

Now, let me write a expression to print few characters. I will take help of substring().

JavaScript Code Test: {{ vueMessage.substring(vueMessage. indexOf("Vue"), vueMessage.length) }}

This will work with the following output:

Fig 2.9: JavaScript substring Example

However, if you write the code with multiple expressions, Vue won't work. Let's see.

JavaScript Code Test: {{

```
        var start = vueMessage.indexOf("Vue")
            end = vueMessage.length;
        vueMessage.substring(start,  end) }}
```

This code does not run, also throws an error on console with a proper explanation.

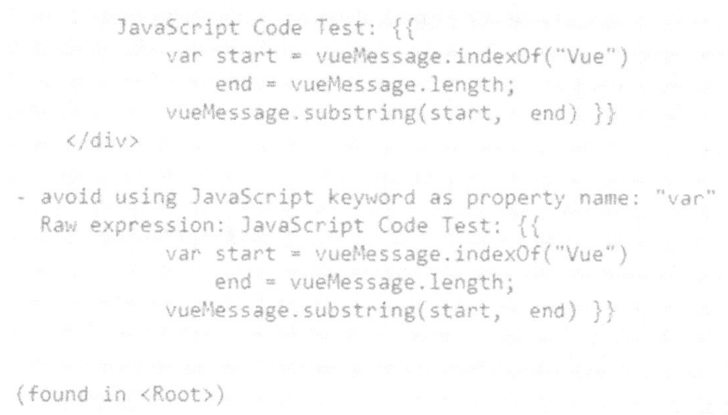

```
JavaScript Code Test: {{
        var start = vueMessage.indexOf("Vue")
            end = vueMessage.length;
        vueMessage.substring(start,  end) }}
    </div>

  - avoid using JavaScript keyword as property name: "var"
    Raw expression: JavaScript Code Test: {{
            var start = vueMessage.indexOf("Vue")
                end = vueMessage.length;
            vueMessage.substring(start,  end) }}


(found in <Root>)
```

Fig 2.10: Error when using multiple expressions with Mustaches

So far, we tested JavaScript expressions with mustaches. Will this work with v- syntax? Let's try.

```
<strong v-html="vueMessage.substring(vueMessage.
indexOf('Vue'), vueMessage.length)"></strong>
```

Perfectly works with a bold message. Following is the output on browser.

```
←  →  C  ⌂    ⓘ File | file:///C:/Users/taditd/Desktop/Vue/vuein7days/Codes/Day2/Basic%20Structure.html

Vue! Love you.
```

Fig 2.11: Substring with v-html Example

Condition and Loop structure

Now that we got a good grasp of basic syntax structure, let's find out how we can add conditional statements and loops.

v-if

Suppose you want to show an image or your profile picture on the web page based on a boolean value. Have a look at the following code:

```
<img v-if="showProfilePic" v-bind:src="profilePicSrc"
height="100px" width="150px" />
```

I have an image tag with **v-if** and **v-bind**. These are called directives. The directive **v-bind** can take another param as the attribute, after the colon. So, **v-bind:src** will bind the value to the **src** attribute of the element.

On the other hand, the v-if directive is used for conditional rendering. As you see the statement **v-if="showProfilePic"**, which is a boolean value that helps to render the element.

Thus, if the value is true, image will be rendered, otherwise, it won't even appear on HTML code. Let's test by setting up some values for this tag.

```
var v1 = new Vue({
            el: "#hello_msg",
            data: {
                    showProfilePic: true,
                    profilePicSrc: "http://taditdash.
                    co.in/wp-content/uploads/2018/06/
                    cropped-Tadit-Dash-Official-Site-2.jpg"
            }
        }
);
```

Here, let's set the **showProfilePic** as true. That will produce the output as the following screenshot.

Fig 2.12: v-if Example with Image

You can see **src** attribute is added and image is shown. Now, let's set **showProfilePic: false.** Bingo! Neither the image is on screen nor the image element.

Fig 2.13: v-if Example with value false

v-else

We learn the way to handle if. Do we have else as well ? Yes, we have an option to work with an else part with this syntax. Instead of showing blank element, let's show one message when we don't want to show the picture.

```
<img v-if="showProfilePic" v-bind:src="profilePicSrc"
height="100px" width="150px" />
<p v-else>Profile Pic can't be shown at the moment!</p>
```

Simple and cute! Take a look at the output:

Fig 2.14: Output

Don't settle here. Let me show you something interesting. Let me change the markup a little bit.

```
<img v-if="showProfilePic" v-bind:src="profilePicSrc"
height="100px" width="150px" />
<p>Just another paragraph!</p>
<p v-else>Profile Pic can't be shown at the moment!</p>
```

We have added another paragraph in between the **v-if** with image and **v-else** with paragraph. Can you guess the output? Here it is:

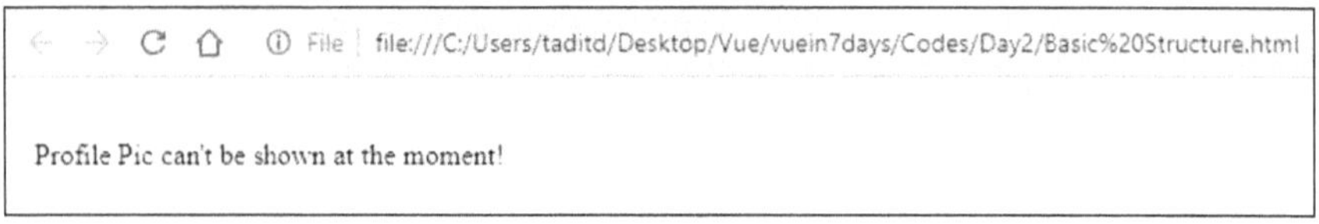

Fig 2.15: *v-else not working due to preceeding paragraph*

As you see from the output, it displays the paragraph content instead of showing the message "Profile Pic can't be shown at the moment!". This means that the **v-else** did not work. And this is by design. It works only when it is followed directly by **v-if** and that's logical, isn't it!

v-else-if

Alright, we explored if and else. Definitely, there would be else-if, isn't it. Let's code that.

```
<strong>Account Type: </strong>
<span v-if="accountType === 1">Super User</span>
<span v-else-if="accountType === 2">Admin</span>
<span v-else>Normal User</span>
```

Let's try to print the account type here. The second span has an attribute **v-else-if**, which acts as **else-if** block. So, if you set **accountType: 2,** the **else-if** will be executed and nothing gets rendered other than the second span.

Like **v-else, v-else-if** also follows the same rule of appearance in the code. That means **v-else-if** should immediately follow either **v-if** or another **v-else-if**. Which implies, **v-else** should either follow **v-if** or a **v-else-if**. If you break this rule, it won't work as expected.

NOTE: v-if, v-else-if, v-else only renders the block/element which is satisfied. That means if you change the value after render in the runtime, then the appropriate element/block gets rendered, otherwise it does not appear on HTML. That is the advantage of conditional rendering.

v-if with <template>

While we saw all examples with single element rendering, what if we want to render a block of elements using **v-if**. Let's do that.

```
<template v-if="accountType === 1">
    <h1>You have Super User with more priviledge!</h1>
    <button>Create Admin</button>
    <button>Delete a User</button>
    <button>Logout</button>
</template>
<template v-else-if="accountType === 2">
    <h1>You are an Admin!</h1>
    <button>Delete a User</button>
    <button>Logout</button>
</template>
<template v-else>
    <h1>You are just a User!</h1>
    <button>Logout</button>
</template>
```

You show different type of menu options to different type of user. I tried to do that using **v-if** and template which helps me to render multiple HTML elements inside a block. In the above example, we have more buttons and priviledges for Super User, which is reduced with other account types.

Reusable Elements

Vue is intelligent enough to reuse elements that are already on DOM, instead of creating more. Let's understand this by one example.

Suppose, we have two textboxes like the following, for different password types.

```
<template v-if="passwordType === 1">
    <label>Enter Password</label>
    <input type="text" placeholder="Enter Password"/>
</template>
<template v-else>
    <label>Enter OTP</label>
    <input type="text" placeholder="Enter OTP"/>
</template>
```

Actual magic happens when you run it. Run and enter some value in the textbox. It would look like following, for **passwordType: 1:**

Fig 2.16: v-if with Template Example

We have a button to toggle the value of **passwordType**. We will learn event handling in the next section, so I am not sharing the code of button for now. Alright, now click on it, you will see the following:

Fig 2.17: v-else rendered without value change

Did you see the magic? The value is still there. However, the label and textbox are changed for OTP. So, the else part got executed, as a result the label and textbox got rendered. However, the value is still there. What does that mean? Simple, that means the textbox, which was initially rendered for **passwordType = 1** got reused. A new textbox is not rendered when you click on the button to toggle the value. That is the beauty of Vue.

Vue intelligently reused the available textbox inside the **v-if** block for **v-else** block. It did not render another textbox. However, it's not required always. Meaning, you might want to render two textboxes for two conditions as you want to operate on them separately or need both of the values at the same time. In that case, you have to explicitly tell Vue not to reuse and render another element instead.

We can do that by adding a **key** attribute.

```
<template v-if="passwordType === 1">
     <label>Enter Password</label>
     <input type="text" placeholder="Enter Password"
     key="text-password" />
</template>
<template v-else>
     <label>Enter OTP</label>
     <input type="text" placeholder="Enter OTP" key="otp-
```

```
password"/>
</template>
```

Now, Vue won't reuse the textbox. It will render new input elements each time you toggle the data **passwordType**. Run this code and feel the difference by following the same steps as you saw above.

v-show

This directive for conditional displaying unlike **v-if** which serves as conditional rendering. They can act as the same if you look at the UI, however, behind the scenes they are significantly different.

While **v-if** does not render the element if condition is false, **v-show** renders the element everytime. It just works on the CSS display property. What that means is, when the condition is false, it makes display false and when true, makes display true. Let's see it in action with an example.

```
<div v-show="showDudeMessage">I am a dude!</div>
```

Setting **showDudeMessage:** true, will produce the following output.

Fig 2.18: v-show Example with value true

Now, let me set it as false. Here is what you will see.

Fig 2.19: v-show Example with value false

Blank output. But, notice the HTML which has a display property set as **none**. That is the main difference between **v-if** and **v-show**. V-show renders the element no matter what the data value is. Just manages the visibility by display property, unlike **v-if**, which renders the element when needed depending on the value.

v-if vs v-show

Now that you know both the directives, it's very easy to identify the differences.

V-if ensures that the element and it's related events are rendered and attached respectively, only when necessary. That is why it is denoted as the "real" conditional rendering. Unlike **v-if, v-show** renders the element always irrespective of data you set it for. It is based upon CSS display toggling.

As **v-if** does not render the element if the condition is false, that means it will render if you toggle the condition and make it true. Which will have a toggle cost because Vue will create the element and insert into DOM. So, don't use **v-if** if you have to toggle the condition frequently. On the other hand, you can use **v-show** if you want to toggle the condition frequently because the element is already rendered, just the display property will be updated. That means it has a higher render cost as the element is always rendered. So, you need to choose wisely according to your project situations.

v-for

As the name suggests, it helps in looping. This directive is used to render list of items in an array or properties of an object. Let's see a simple example where we can render menus with **v-for**.

```
<ul>
    <li v-for="menu in menus">{{ menu }}</li>
</ul>
```

Where menu can be defined as:

```
var v1 = new Vue({
    el: "#hello_msg",
    data: {
        menus: [ "Home", "About", "Contact" ]
    }
});
```

Here **menus** is an array with menu items. Output produced is something like the following:

Fig 2.20: v-for Example with Navigation Links

Now, let's work with an array of objects instead.

```
var v1 = new Vue({
    el: "#hello_msg",
    authors: [
            { Id: 1, Name: "Vishal Jain" },
            { Id: 2, Name: "Nirmal Hota" },
            { Id: 3, Name: "Tadit Dash" }
    ]
});
```

To render the UI, we can write like the following with a **div** which packs the divs designed for object properties. The code is pretty easy to understand where I am trying to print the Author Id and Name properties one by one.

```
<div v-for="author in authors">
    <div><strong>Author Id:</strong> {{ author.Id }}</div>
```

```
<div><strong>Author Name:</strong> {{ author.Name }}</div>
</div>
```

This will produce the following output:

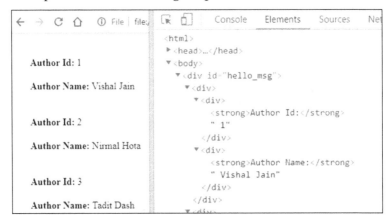

Fig 2.21: v-for with Array of Objects

We have shown one div of rendered HTML at the right side. You can see the properties are rendered inside one one divs along with a container div (rendered with help of **v-for**) which packages the whole thing.

You can design the same kind of UI using templates as we did in v-if. Let's do that and see what happens. Code would look like the following:

```
<template v-for="author in authors">
    <div><strong>Author Id:</strong> {{ author.Id }}</div>
    <div><strong>Author Name:</strong> {{ author.Name }}</div>
</template>
```

And the output is little bit different:

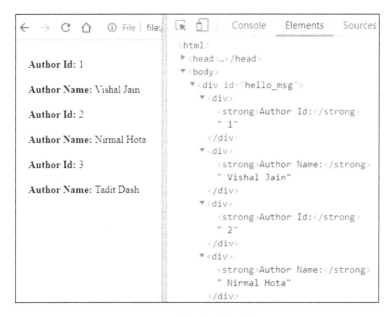

Fig 2.22: v-for with Templates

Did you notice the change? See how the extra parent **div** is eliminated because we no longer have that parent **div**. We have template which directly renders the children.

v-for with v-if

Both can be used on the same node and it becomes useful when you want to conditionally restrict/allow some items while iterating. Let's see one example to understand.

```
<template v-for="author in authors" v-if="author.Id > 1">
        <div><strong>Author Id:</strong> {{ author.Id }}</div>
        <div><strong>Author Name:</strong> {{ author.Name }}</div>
</template>
```

This would produce the following output:

Fig 2.23: v-for with v-if Example

We could be able to restrict the rendering of one item with the condition **author.Id > 1** with a **v-if** directive.

Another way to use **v-if** with **v-for** is to conditionally render the whole **v-for** block. Let's have a look.

```
<div v-if="authors.length">
        <template v-for="author in authors" v-if="author.Id > 1">
            <div><strong>Author Id:</strong> {{ author.Id }}</div>
            <div><strong>Author Name:</strong> {{ author.Name
            }}</div>
        </template>
</div>
```

Whole author list is rendered only when the authors array contains some objects. Otherwise, nothing is rendered.

Keys and Index

While operating with Objects, we can get the property names and indices easily. Let's modify our code to print out the key instead of hard coding them like Author Id and Author Name.

```
<div v-for="author in authors">
        <template v-for="(value, key) in author">
            <span><strong>{{ key }}:</strong> {{ value }} </
            span>
        </template>
</div>
```

Here we have two **v-for** directives one after another, as we wanted to iterate through the properties of the object which is **author**.

Notice the change in the v-for directive part in the second loop, that is **v-for="(value, key) in author"**, which helps to get the value and key from the object. Value and keys are nothing but the property value and property name. Output would make it clear, take a look at it :

Fig 2.24: v-for with Key

It printed the property name and value iteratively for each object in the array. We no more have any hard coded property names.

Moreover, you can also get the index of the property. Just need to update the code a little bit.

```
<div v-for="author in authors">
      <template v-for="(value, key, index) in author">
            <span><strong>(Index: {{ index }}), {{ key
            }}:</strong> {{ value }} </span>
      </template>
</div>
```

Now the change is to include index in the declaration as **v-for="(value, key, index) in author"**. This would produce the following output:

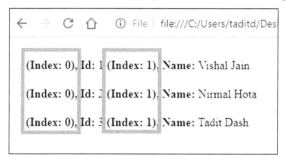

Fig 2.25: v-for with index

You can see that for each property, we can easily get the index for it. Therefore, for each object, index for Id property is 0 and Name property is 1.

Form elements and basic event handling

In this section, we will move gradually towards binding values with form elements like textbox, textarea, radio buttons, checkboxes, and so on. Then event handling is what we need to interact with the form elements so that we can bring some dynamicity to the application.

Form Elements

Alright, let's explore one by one starting with simple textbox.

Textbox

Upto this point, we learnt how we can bind data to the elements using **v-bind**. So, for **input type="text"**, we can write something like this.

```
<input type="text" v-bind:value="email" placeholder="Enter
email id" />
```

No doubt, this will work. However, if you use the data property **email** anywhere in the JavaScript code, you won't be able to get the updated value. Meaning, when you start typing inside the box, the data won't get updated. We can easily verify this by printing the data on another element. Let's see the code.

```
<input type="text" v-bind:value="email" placeholder="Enter
email id" />
<p>Your Email Id: {{ email }}</p>
```

So, here we are printing the data inside a paragraph. You can initialize the value to something inside the Vue object. Let's see what happens on the output:

Fig 2.26: One Way Data Binding (TextBox v-bind not updating Vue data value)

You can notice, we have typed an email id, but it is not printing inside the paragraph. Looks like *One-Way Data Binding,* isn't it. You set the value and then forget. To make this happen, we can add one input event (we will learn even in details in the next session). Let's add the event.

```
<input type="text" v-bind:value="email" v-on:input="email
= $event.target.value" placeholder="Enter email id" />
```

Notice the **v-on:input** event, which is responsible for updating the typed data to the email property. Now, the message would be shown as you type. Here is the output:

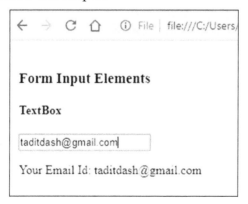

Fig 2.27: Two Way Data Binding (TextBox v-bind v-on updating the Vue data value)

This is called *Two-Way Data Binding.* In Vue, this can be simplified by using **v-model** directive instead of using **v-bind** and **v-on**. Let's see how.

```
<input type="text" v-model="email" placeholder="Enter email
id" />
<p>Your Email Id: {{ email }}</p>
```

This will work exactly the same as above. This is syntax sugar as it simplifies the code to a large extent and handles all events for input.

Note: There is an interesting thing to note here with **v-model.** Vue won't take the value inside the markup if you provide for initial load. It will always assume that you have given the value in data property inside Vue object. Otherwise, it will ignore anything mentioned on the HTML.

Textarea

The same thing applies for Textarea too. Let's code.

```
<textarea v-model="profileBio" placeholder="Add your
biography"></textarea>
<p>Your Bio: {{ profileBio }}</p>
```

This would produce the following output:

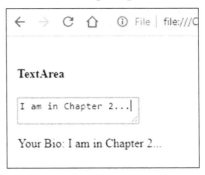

Fig 2.28: Textarea Example with v-model

Checkbox

Like the above two cases, let's code for Checkbox.

```
<input type="checkbox" id="cbTerms"
v-model="isTermsAccepted">
<label for="cbTerms">{{ isTermsAccepted ? "Terms accepted":
"Terms not accepted" }}</label>
```

Here we have one Checkbox for *Terms Acceptance* and the value is used on another label. If value is true, we will print *Terms accepted,* else *Terms not accepted*. When you run and check the checkbox, it would display the following screenshot:

Fig 2.29: *Checkbox Rendered with v-model*

Checkboxes are mostly used to take multiple selection. We can easily manage the selections using a single array, which can store all the data. For instance, in a typical form, we might ask the customers to select their notification preferences.

```
<input type="checkbox" id="cbSms" value="SMS"
v-model="notificationMethods">
<label for="cbSms">SMS</label>
<input type="checkbox" id="cbEmail" value="Email"
v-model="notificationMethods">
<label for="cbEmail">Email</label>
<input type="checkbox" id="cbVoice" value="Voice"
v-model="notificationMethods">
<label for="cbVoice">Voice</label>
<div>You will be notified by these methods: <span>{{
notificationMethods }}</span></div>
```

I have three checkboxes for different type of notification method. Each checkbox is attached with an appropriate value. Notice the v-model directive value in all checkboxes which is **notification Methods.** That means every checkbox is going to store their value in this data array. For this work, we need to declare this as an array.

```
var v1 = new Vue({
            el: "#hello_msg",
            data: {
                  notificationMethods: []
            }
      }
   );
```

The output will be something like below, if you select the **SMS** and **Email** option.

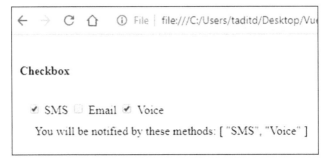

Fig 2.30: Multiple Selection with Checkboxes

Radio Button

Radio buttons are used for single selection. Selecting **Gender** on a form is the most common example for radio button.

```
<input type="radio" id="rMale" value="Male"
v-model="gender">
<label for="rMale">Male</label>
<br>
<input type="radio" id="rFemale" value="Female"
v-model="gender">
<label for="rFemale">Female</label>
<div>You are a {{ gender }}.</div>
```

Like checkbox, here we are attaching the **v-model** with the same data property, however, this won't be an array. It will be a simple string.

```
var v1 = new Vue({
        el: "#hello_msg",
        data: {
                gender: ""
        }
    }
);
```

This produces the following output, if you select **Female** option:

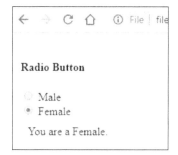

Fig 2.31: RadioButtons with v-model

DropDowns (Select)

Following on, let's code for a dropdownlist.

```
<select v-model="country">
      <option value="">Select country</option>
      <option>India</option>
      <option>Nepal</option>
      <option>Sri Lanka</option>
      <option>Australia</option>
</select>
<span>You are from {{ country }}.</span>
```

The Vue declaration will look as following:

```
var v1 = new Vue({
          el: "#hello_msg",
          data: { country: "" }
     });
```

We have added a span to print the country. Here is the output:

Fig 2.32: Dropdownlist with v-model

For multiselect, we need to add an attribute to the select tag and change the data type to an array. Let's code first.

```
<select v-model="skills" multiple>
        <option>Vue</option>
        <option>Angular</option>
        <option>React</option>
        <option>Node</option>
</select>
<p>You have skills: {{ skills }}.</p>
```

Notice the attribute **multiple** added to the select tag. Now the declaration part. We have to declare the data as an array.

```
var v1 = new Vue({
            el: "#hello_msg",
            data: {        skills: [] }
});
```

Have a look at the output as well:

Fig 2.33: Multiselect Dropdownlist with v-model

As of now, we talked about hard coded options. Now suppose you are going to render options by getting them from an api or database. That means dynamic options. Let's see how we can easily bind them to the UI.

Cities can be an array like below and selectedCity will hold the value of the city which we will select from dropdown. I am still hard coding everything in the code, however it is just for the sake of demonstration. In actual project, you will get these records from database or an API.

```
var v1 = new Vue({
            el: "#hello_msg",
            data: {
                cities: [
                        { text: "Bhubaneswar", value: "1" },
                        { text: "Delhi", value: "2" },
                        { text: "Mumbai", value: "3" },
                        { text: "Pune", value: "4" }
                ],
                selectedCity: ""
            }
        }
);
```

Now, the UI part would look like as follows :

```
<select v-model="selectedCity">
        <option v-for="city in cities" v-bind:value="city.
value">{{ city.text }}</option>
</select>
<span>You are from city: {{ selectedCity }}.</span>
```

Notice the **option** tag where we have **v-for** directive which helps us to loop through the **cities** array. As we have a value attribute in **option** tag, we can bind that using **v-bind** directive and then show the text with mustaches.

When you select Bhubaneswar, it would print 1, as shown in the following screenshot:

Fig 2.34: v-bind with value for options in Dropdownlist

Note: The **v-bind** directive helps us to bind dynamic value to the elements. If you see in the above example, **v-bind:value="city.value"**

allowed us to bind non-string values as the declared cities array have integers 1, 2, 3, 4 in it.

Basic Event Handling

The directive v-on can be used to bind events to the HTML elements. A simple click event for a button can be like this:

```
<button v-on:click="SubmitForm">Submit</button>
```

You can define the event inside the Vue object as:

```
var v1 = new Vue({
            el: "#hello_msg",
            methods: {
                    SubmitForm: function() {
                            alert("Hey man");
                    },
            }
);
```

We can pass data easily to the events like this:

```
<button v-on:click="SubmitForm('We are going to submit
the form)">Submit</button>
```

Which can be caught inside the event as follows:

```
SubmitForm: function(message) {
        alert(message);
}
```

Now let's talk about change event on a textbox.

```
<input type="text" v-on:change="AlertText">
```

The event can be defined as:

```
AlertText: function(event) {
        alert(event.target.value);
}
```

Today we explored how we can structure a page using basic syntaxes of Vue. Mustaches is the basic syntax which is very easy to use and has all that flexibility to display data on HTML elements.

However, Mustaches syntax has some limitations which can be overcome by Vue directives. We started with v-bind directive to attach data to HTML attributes and then we explored another directive called v-html to bind data to the HTML property directly.

Going ahead we learnt more directives like v-if, v-else, v-else-if and v-show for conditional rendering of elements. We had a deep insights of those directives which helps us to select them at appropriate situations.

To render list or an array of elements, Vue provides us v-for directive and it can be combindely used with v-if when we want to restrict some items in the list.

After all these directives, finally it was time to deal with form elements like TextBox, TextArea, CheckBox, Radio Button and Dropdowns. That is where we came across v-model directive for two way data binding.

Last, but not the least, we had a quick overview of handling basic events like click and change with Vue.

In the next chapter, we will move towards advanced topics like computed property and watchers.

DAY 3
Computed Property

In the previous chapter, we have made our hands dirty with the VueJS code in HTML pages. We learnt the way to declare and display the variables on screen. The conditional control of DOM element rendering, flow of control structure, event and data binding, we have learnt so far.

In this chapter, we will go one step ahead with VueJS. We will look into the computed properties, why they are needed, how they can be utilized along with the watchers. By the end of the topic, you would be aware of use of both computed property and watcher. We will try to draw a comparison between those two.

The last lesson was to teach the way to define the data attributes in the Vue object. Data attributes works as the data holders and transmitters while we are dealing with the Vue object. In the Vue enabled DOM, data attributes take the input and keeps rendering it in that DOM.

We will begin this day by solving a simple problem in a simple way with the help of Vue. We will keep refactoring the solution in order to move ahead with learning.

Greetings to the user

Let's greet our user with a simple message. User needs to enter their first and last name. We will greet them with their full name.

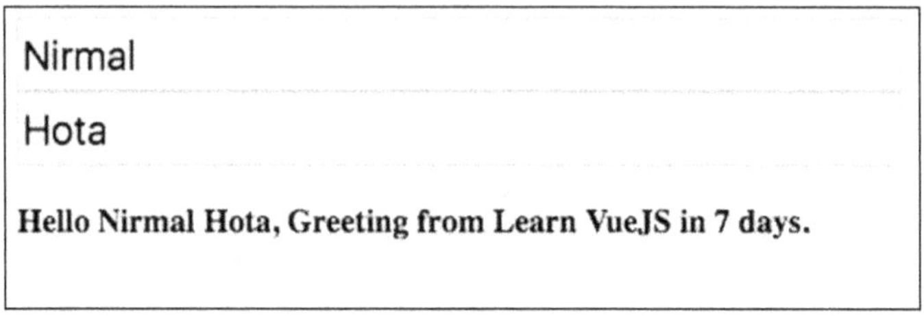

Nirmal
Hota
Hello Nirmal Hota, Greeting from Learn VueJS in 7 days.

Fig 3.1: UI to take user name input and greet the user

Approach

We need to take two data attributes to accept first name and last name. Both the first name and last name needs to get concatenated to form the full name and display the greeting message below to the inputs.

We will follow the simple approach by writing a method to concatenate the inputs. The same method will cater the value in the display string directly. That's the easy and quickest solutions.

Let's check how the code looks like

```html
<!DOCTYPE html >
<html>
    <head>
        <script  src="https://cdn.jsdelivr.net/npm/vue/dist/
        vue.js"></script>
        <style>
            input[type=text]{
                width: 50%;
                height: 30px;
                font-size: 20px;
            };
        </style>
    </head>
    <body>
```

```
<div id="app_div">
    <input type="text" v-model="first_name"
    placeHolder="First name"/> <br>
    <input type="text" v-model="last_name"
    placeHolder="Last name"/>
<br/><br/>
    <b v-show="get_full_name() !=' '">Hello {{ get_
    full_name() }}, Greeting from Learn VueJS in 7
    days.</b>
</div>
<script>
    var app = new Vue({
        el: "#app_div",
        data: {
            first_name: '',
            last_name: '',
        },
        methods: {
            get_full_name : function(){
                return this.first_name + ' ' + this.last_
                name;
            },
        }
    });
</script>
</body>
</html>
```

We have taken two data properties to hold the user inputs and associated them with the input texts.

- **first_name**
- **last_name**

The method **get_full_name** in the Vue object, concatenates both the variables along with an additional space in between them and returns the full name, which gets printed on screen in the greet message. We have used **v-show** directive, so that it won't render the greeting message when there is no first name and last name specified in the screen.

It works !!

So, what are the drawbacks here?

It would be memory consuming. When we call this method to show the greeting message, it will try creating the full stack and allocate memory to it. So, each time we make changes in the **first_name** or **last_name** data attribute, it will call that method, which results a lot of memory allocation to same method for each instance.

Imagine the scenario, a method involving more calculations and/or processing would lower down the performance of the app as well as consumes more memory.

Let's talk about the solution

We can use the computed property to address this problem. Unlike the method approach above, computed property will cache the result. It won't get refreshed, unless the dependent v-models get changed.

```
1    <!DOCTYPE html >
2    <html>
3        <head>
4            <script src="https://cdn.jsdelivr.net/npm/vue/dist/vue.js"></script>
5            <style>
6                input[type=text]{
7                    width: 50%;
8                    height: 30px;
9                    font-size: 20px;
10               };
11
12           </style>
13       </head>
14       <body>
15           <div id="app_div">
16               <input type="text" v-model="first_name" placeHolder="First name"/> <br>
17               <input type="text" v-model="last_name" placeHolder="Last name"/>        <br/><br/>
18               <b v-show="full_name != ''">Hello {{ full_name }} Greeting from Learn VueJS in 7 days.</b>
19           </div>
20           <script>
21               var app = new Vue({
22                   el: "#app_div",
23                   data: {
24                       first_name: '',
25                       last_name: '',
26                   },
27                   computed: {
28                       full_name : function(){
29                           return this.first_name + ' ' + this.last_name;
30                       },
31                   }
32               });
33           </script>
34       </body>
35
36   </html>
37
```

Fig 3.2: Code using computed property

Now we have refactored the existing code. Mainly we did two things.

- We have removed the method attribute and added the computed attribute.
- We don't need the parenthesis for using the computed attribute in the page unlike the method.

How this will be the solution?

Computed properties get cached. So, when for the first time both the model variables i.e. **first_name** and **last_name** get some input, the computed property gets its value. It gets cached after that until the model variables gets a new value.

The advantage of using the computed property is as follows,

- It gets cached
- No changes to the value until the depended models get changed
- It is ready to use from the cache
- Performs faster than the methods

Computed Property versus Method

The basic and the biggest difference between the computed property and method is their execution upon usage. In other words, methods get executed each time it is called, whereas the computed property uses the cache unless the dependency gets changed.

Let's try with a timestamp value

Let's create a method and computed property. Each of them should return the current timestamp so that we can mark the difference between the values.

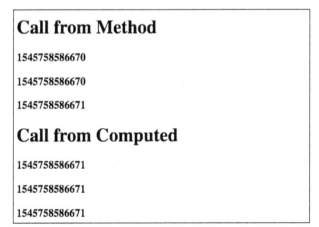

Call from Method

1545758586670

1545758586670

1545758586671

Call from Computed

1545758586671

1545758586671

1545758586671

Fig 3.3: Output comparison between the method and computed property with timestamp

In the above image, we have shown the output of our program. The up ones are the result from the method calls and the lower ones are from computed property.

The timestamps in the method section has the difference in the values, although we are calling the same method. That means, the same method is getting called again and again to get the value. But in the computed property section values will always be same as the value with the first call, as it fetches the value from the cache. In the first call, the generate value i.e. Current timestamp in this case, gets stored in the cache. Upon subsequent calls, the value only gets fetched and displayed from cache unless the page gets refreshed. On refresh, it changes the value of the computed property, as this computed property depends on the timestamps.

With multiple refresh of the screen, we can see the method values may be same or different, depending upon the execution time. But the computed property value will always be the same.

```
<!DOCTYPE html >
<html>
    <head>
        <script src="https://cdn.jsdelivr.net/npm/vue/dist/
        vue.js"></script>
    </head>
    <body>
        <div id="app_div">
                <h1>Call from Method</h1>
                        <h3>{{ nowMethod() }}</h3>
                        <h3>{{ nowMethod() }}</h3>
                        <h3>{{ nowMethod() }}</h3>
                <h1>Call from Computed</h1>
                        <h3>{{ nowComputed }}</h3>
                        <h3>{{ nowComputed }}</h3>
                        <h3>{{ nowComputed }}</h3>
        </div>
        <script>
            var app = new Vue({
                el: "#app_div",
                methods: {
                    nowMethod : function(){
                        return Date.now();
                    },
```

```
            },
            computed: {
                nowComputed : function(){
                    return Date.now();
                },
            }
        });
    </script>
  </body>
</html>
```

Getters and setters in the computed property

The computed property looks like a normal attribute in the HTML page. Then the natural question that arises in our thoughts, *is it possible to use getters and setters with computed property?*

The answer is YES.

We can define the getters and setters for the computed properties as well.

Getter

When we say, return the value to the computed property, it works on the getter so that we can retrieve the value from the particular computed property.

Let's try this

We will take the same example as above; we will only need to show our user if the value is Manually Edited or Automatically Combined.

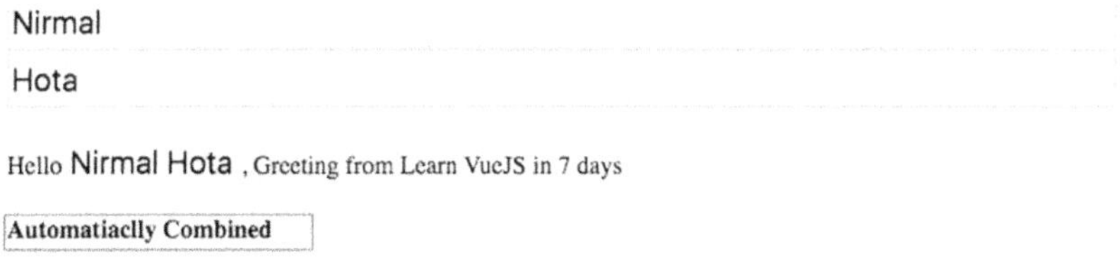

Nirmal

Hota

Hello **Nirmal Hota** , Greeting from Learn VueJS in 7 days

Automatiaclly Combined

Fig 3.4: Getter example to show strings combined automatically

In this UI, the **first name** and **last name** are combined to create the full name. As mentioned in the last example, we have used the **full_name** as a computed property and hold the combined value to display the same on screen. As mentioned earlier, this combination of value is being returned by the **getter** method.

As marked in the red rectangle in the above image, it says **Automatically Combined**.

Setter

Now, let's use the setter method and we will notify the user, if the value is manually edited. In other words, if the full name directly gets changed by the user, it will display the message that the value is **Manually Edited**.

Let's try this

In the same example, we will show the message as manually edited as shown in the following image within the red rectangle.

Fig 3.5: Setter example to show string edited manually

Explain the UI Elements

In the above screens (both Getter and Setter UI), we have taken three inputs for **first_name, last_name** and **full_name** (the computed property). The only difference between the first two input boxes and the last input box is, in the last input box, i.e. the **full_name** input box, we have applied the styles to reduce its width and remove its border.

style="width: 110px; border: 0px;"

Let's look into that piece of code

```
computed: {
    full_name : {
            get: function(){
            this.is_combined = true;
            return this.first_name + ' ' +
            this.last_name;
        },
        set: function(value){
            this.is_combined = false;
        }
    }
}
```

As shown in the image, we have defined the **get** and **set** methods for the **full_name** computed property.

In the get method, we did following:

- We have returned the combined value of the **first_name** and **last_name** to create the computed attribute
- Set the **is_combined** variable to **true**

In the **set** method, we did following

- Set the **is_combined** variable to **false**

Whenever the **get** method gets called to display the value, it will set the **is_combined** to true by showing the **Automatically Combined** message to the user and **sets** false when set method is called by showing the Manually edited message.

Here, **set** method will be called as soon as we edit the **full_name** in the input box specified.

The full view of the code looks like the following:

```
<!DOCTYPE html >
<html>
    <head>
        <script src="https://cdn.jsdelivr.net/npm/
        vue/dist/vue.js"></script>
        <style>
          input[type=text]{
            width: 50%;
```

```
                height: 30px;
                font-size: 20px;
        };

    </style>
  </head>
  <body>
    <div id="app_div">
            <input type="text" v-model="first_name"
            placeHolder="First name"/> <br>
            <input type="text" v-model="last_name"
            placeHolder="Last name"/> <br/><br/>
    Hello <input type="text" v-model="full_name"
    placeHolder="Full name" style="width: 110px; border:
    0px;"/>, Greeting from Learn VueJS in 7 days
    <br/><br/>
            <b>{{ is_combined ? "Automatiaclly Combined":
            "Manually edited"  }}</b>
            </div>
            <script>
                var app = new Vue({
                    el: "#app_div",
                    data: {
                            first_name: 'Nirmal',
                            last_name: 'Hota',
                    is_combined: true
                        },
                        computed: {
                            full_name : {
                        get: function(){
                            this.is_combined = true;
                             return this.first_name + ' ' + this.
                            last_name;
                                },
                                set: function(value){
                                    this.is_combined = false;
                                }
                            }
                        }
                    }
                });
            </script>
        </body>
    </html>
```

Watched property

Watched property is used to watch the variable changes and execute the code blocks written underneath.

Let's take an example

We will build a *liter conversion calculator*. As a part of the *liter conversion calculator*, we will take an input text, which will take the number of liters as input. As soon as the user enters the value, the milliliter conversion of the same will get calculated and displayed in the input box next to it. User will also get the liter conversion of the milliliter when enters the milliliter value in the input box.

How the output looks like

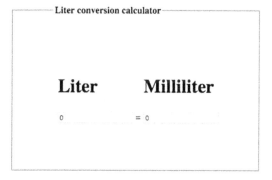

Fig 3.6: Liter conversion calculator

As shown in the screenshot, liter value entered in the **Liter** text box will display the **Milliliter** equivalent of the same and vice versa.

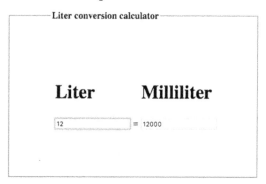

Fig 3.7: Liter conversion calculator with values

As shown in the screenshot, we have entered the liter value and milliliter value is also getting changed immediately.

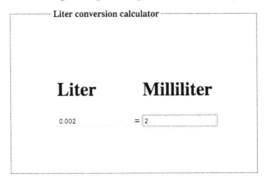

Fig 3.8: Liter conversion calculator with values

Similarly, enter values in the milliliter input, calculate and displays the liter value immediately.

Explain the code

In the HTML part, we have used the table layout design structure for our convention. Div layout can be used to prepare the tabular structure of inputs.

VueJS supports **watch** label to define the watched properties. Since we need to accept the inputs, then we need to define the model variables to get the data in it. So, we have defined two model variables **liter** and **milliliter**, inside the **data** block. The same variables are used in the input fields in the **v-model** attribute to accept the input values in them.

```
watch: {
    liter: function(val){
        this.liter = val;
        this.mliter = val *1000;
    },
    mliter: function(val){
        this.liter = val/1000;
        this.mliter = val;
    },
},
```

Same as Model variable names

Fig 3.9: Defining watchers

Now, we need to add the watch to the same attributes, so that we can see the value changes, and execute the code blocks immediately. In order to add the watch to the same model variables, we need to use the same variable names to define the watch.

Watch properties code block fires as soon as the change happens or the conditions met, as defined in the watch label block. It keeps watching the **v-model** variable to take the effect of the change.

```
<!DOCTYPE html >
<html>
   <head>
      <script src="https://cdn.jsdelivr.net/npm/vue/dist/
      vue.js"></script>
   </head>
   <body>
   <div id="app_div">
            <fieldset style="width: 20%; padding: 5%">
                <legend style="font-weight: bold">Liter
                conversion calculator</legend>
                <table>
                    <tr>
                        <td><h1>Liter</h1></td>
                        <td></td>
                        <td><h1>Milliliter</h1></td>
                    </tr>
                    <tr>
                        <td><input type="text"
                        v-model="liter"/></td>
                        <td> = </td>
                        <td><input type="text"
                        v-model="mliter"/></td>
                    </tr>
                </table>
            </fieldset>
   </div>
   <script>
      var app = new Vue({
         el: "#app_div",
                data: {
                                        liter: 0,
                                        mliter: 0
                },
         watch: {
```

```
                        liter: function(val){
                            this.liter = val;
                            this.mliter = val *1000;
                        },
                        mliter: function(val){
                            this.liter = val/1000;
                            this.mliter = val;
                        },
                    },
                });
            </script> </body>
        </html>
```

Watchers more in use

In the reactive environment, watchers play a great role as it keeps watching the properties, it can react as per the action defined.

Watcher not only keeps watching the property, it also keeps track of the old and new values of the attributes. It caches the current value. Upon change, watcher returns the value as old value and the changed value as the new value. Again caches the new value as the current value.

As shown in the previous example, **watchers** get defined under the watch hook of the vue object. As a thumb rule, the watcher names must be same as the name of the attribute to be watched.

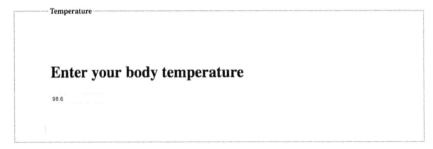

Fig 3.10: Body temperature calculator

We have used a watch property here to capture the body temperature, which is initialized to 98.6. User enters the current body temperature. Depending upon the old and new values it will display the message.

```
watch: {
    temperature: function(newValue, oldValue){
        if(newValue < oldValue){
            this.temp_message = "Your temperature is dropping.";
        }
        else if(newValue > oldValue){
            this.temp_message = "Your temperature is rising.";
        }
        else{
            this.temp_message = "Your temperature is still unchanged.";
        }
    }
},
```

Fig 3.11: Managing temperature watch to return value as per the values

We have attached the watcher with the **temperature** model variable. If the **newValue** of the temperature is less than the **oldValue**, then it will display the message **Your temperature is dropping**. The output message gets assigned to the **temp_message** model variable.

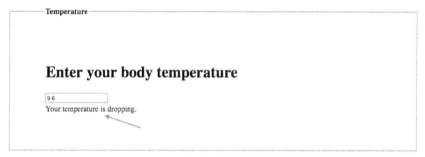

Fig 3.12: Temperature calculator showing the dropping of value

If **newValue** is greater than the **oldValue**, then the message would be **Your temperature is rising.**

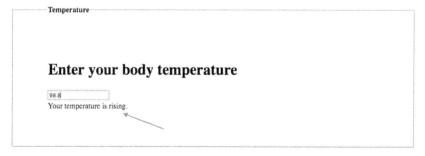

Fig 3.13: Temperature calculator showing rising value

If they both remain same, then the user would see the message as **Your temperature is still unchanged**.

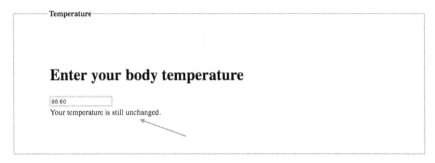

Fig 3.14: *Temperature calculator reverting back to value unchanged*

How it works?

User enters the temperature value in the text box. As soon as the value gets changed in the text box, it changes the value of the **temperature** model variable. Since the watcher is applied on the temperature, it starts executing the code block written in the watch.

```
<!DOCTYPE html >
<html>
    <head>
        <script src="https://cdn.jsdelivr.net/npm/vue/dist/
        vue.js"></script>
    </head>
    <body>
        <div id="app_div">
            <fieldset style="width: 50%; padding: 5%">
                <legend style="font-weight:
                bold">Temperature</legend>
                <table>
                    <tr>
                        <td><h1>Enter your body temperature
                        </h1></td>
                    </tr>
                    <tr>
                        <td><input type="text"
                        v-model="temperature"/> </td>
                    </tr>
                    <tr>
```

```
                <td><span>{{ temp_message }}</
                span></td>
            </tr>
        </table>
    </fieldset>
</div>
<script>
    var app = new Vue({
        el: "#app_div",
            data: {
                temperature: 98.6,
                temp_message: "",
            },
        watch: {
                temperature: function(newValue,
                oldValue){
                    if(newValue < oldValue){
                        this.temp_message = "Your
                        temperature is dropping.";
                    }
                    else if(newValue > oldValue){
                        this.temp_message = "Your
                        temperature is rising.";
                    }
                    else{
                        this.temp_message = "Your
                        temperature is still
                        unchanged.";
                    }
                }
        },
    });
</script>
</body>
</html>
```

Watcher on computed property

Computed properties are also like other model attributes, which can hold values with some extra computed capability. As discussed earlier, we can also do get and set values in it.

Now the obvious question we have, can we apply watcher on the computed property? The answer is a big YES.

Like other model attributes, we can make watchers watch to the computed property as well. It can track the changes in the computed property and behave as per the codes written in it.

We will extend the same temperature meter. We will add Fahrenheit conversion of the Celsius.

Fig 3.15: *Celsius to Fahrenheit conversion calculator*

We have added a new computed property called **ftemperature**, to calculate the Fahrenheit from the Celsius. Watcher will be added to the same computed property to watch the changes in the values. As soon as the value in the Celsius text box gets changed, it gets the computed property calculated for the Fahrenheit. This change will get observed by the watcher and executes the code written inside.

```
<script>
    var app = new Vue({
        el: "#app_div",
                data: {
                    temperature: 98.6,
                    temp_message: "",
                    f_message: ""
                },
                computed: {
                    ftemperature: function(){
                        return (this.temperature * 9/5) + 32;
                    }
                },
        watch: {
                temperature: function(newValue, oldValue){
                        if(newValue < oldValue){
```

```
                        this.temp_message = "Your
                        temperature is dropping.";
                }
                else if(newValue > oldValue){
                        this.temp_message = "Your
                        temperature is rising.";
                }
                else{
                        this.temp_message = "Your
                        temperature is still
                        unchanged.";
                }
            },
        ftemperature: function(newValue, oldValue){
                this.f_message = "Temperature changed from
                " + oldValue + " fahrenheit to " +
                newValue + " fahrenheit";
                }
        },
    });
</script>
```

So the change of the Celsius value will compute the Fahrenheit value and get stored in the **ftemperature**.

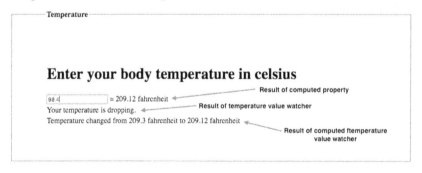

Fig 3.16: *Celsius to Fahrenheit conversion calculator functionality*

With this change, it is obvious that, both Celsius and Fahrenheit value will get the change effect. The same effect will be watched by the watcher and the code block inside both the watch properties i.e. **temperature** and **ftemperature** to display the message gets executed.

In this chapter, we have covered the computed property and the watchers. We discussed how the computed properties work from caches which are different than a normal method call. Method gets called on each call, whereas computed properties gets called from the cache unless there is a change in the dependent model variables. We have also seen the way to use get and set with the computed properties.

We discussed VueJS watchers are also very useful tool to watch any property to handle the live changes. Watchers also return the old and new values on change of the value. We can also apply watchers on the computed properties as well.

In the next chapter, we will discuss on the basics of VueJs components, registering the components and defining the component properties. Components are the re-usable entities supported by Vue.

DAY 4

Components

In the previous chapter, we learnt the way to create computed property. We also explored the way to apply get and set in the computed property. The comparison between method and computed property helped us to know the advantages of the computed properties.

We also made our hands our dirty with the watchers. We also learnt getting the old and current value of a control using the watcher.

In this chapter, we will cover the basics of components. We will see, why we need a component, how we can create, register and use a component. We will also define props with the component to see how they really function.

Use controls repeatedly

We keep using inputs to get the user data from the user. Same kind of fields need to be reused in many places in our project. Let's consider an ecommerce application, which uses the addresses in many place. We need addresses for contact, billing, shipping, and so on.

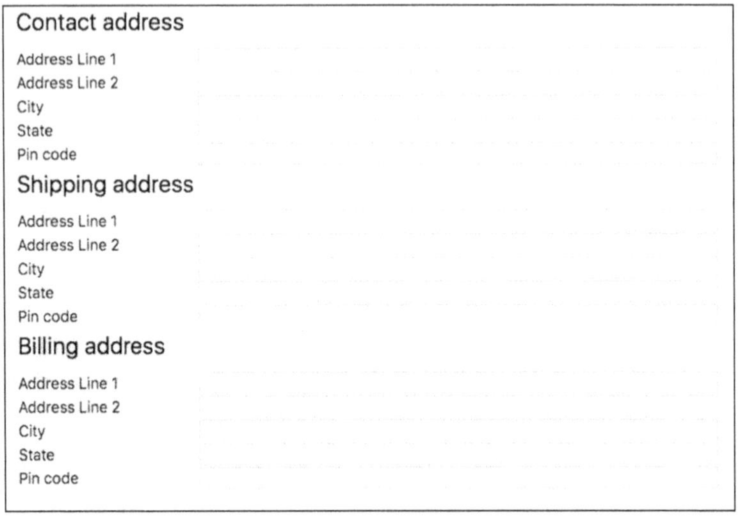

Contact address

Address Line 1
Address Line 2
City
State
Pin code

Shipping address

Address Line 1
Address Line 2
City
State
Pin code

Billing address

Address Line 1
Address Line 2
City
State
Pin code

Fig 4.1: Addresses with repeated controls

The same user input controls need to use multiple times in a repeated manner to collect the data. So, we need to copy and paste the same set of inputs each time we need to collect the address data from the user.

```html
<fieldset class="container">
    <legend>Contact address</legend>
    <div class="row">
        <div class="col-2">Address Line 1</div>
        <div class="col-6"><input type="text" class="full-width" v-model="contact_address_line1" /></div>
    </div>
    <div class="row">
        <div class="col-2">Address Line 2</div>
        <div class="col-6"><input type="text" class="full-width" v-model="contact_address_line2" /></div>
    </div>
    <div class="row">
        <div class="col-2">City</div>
        <div class="col-6"><input type="text" class="full-width" v-model="contact_city" /></div>
    </div>
    <div class="row">
        <div class="col-2">State</div>
        <div class="col-6"><input type="text" class="full-width" v-model="contact_state" /></div>
    </div>
    <div class="row">
        <div class="col-2">Pin code</div>
        <div class="col-6"><input type="text" class="full-width" v-model="contact_pincode" /></div>
    </div>
</fieldset>
<fieldset class="container">
    <legend>Shipping address</legend>
    <div class="row">
        <div class="col-2">Address Line 1</div>
        <div class="col-6"><input type="text" class="full-width" v-model="shipping_address_line1" />
        </div>
    </div>
    <div class="row">
        <div class="col-2">Address Line 2</div>
        <div class="col-6"><input type="text" class="full-width" v-model="shipping_address_line2" />
        </div>
    </div>
    <div class="row">
        <div class="col-2">City</div>
        <div class="col-6"><input type="text" class="full-width" v-model="shipping_city" /></div>
    </div>
    <div class="row">
        <div class="col-2">State</div>
        <div class="col-6"><input type="text" class="full-width" v-model="shipping_state" /></div>
    </div>
    <div class="row">
        <div class="col-2">Pin code</div>
        <div class="col-6"><input type="text" class="full-width" v-model="shipping_pincode" /></div>
    </div>
</fieldset>
```

Fig 4.2: Code for the repeated address control

Not only copy and paste the same control, we also need to have repeated set of model variables for each of the controls. As shown in the image, same **address_line1** needs to be defined for the contact, shipping, billing addresses, and so on. This creates a lot of repeated codes and reduces the readability which puts the code maintenance in risk situation.

How to avoid such situations?

Component is the answer here. We need to have components to avoid these repetitions in code.

What is component?

Components are the vue instances which can be reused to perform certain task. They can be reused in multiple places by just instantiating the same.

We will design our first component

We will see how really a component gets designed. We will also see the way to render a component in page.

To start, first, let's design a component to render a text box along with a label on screen. We will reuse the same to render multiple.

```
<!DOCTYPE html >
<html>
    <head>
        <meta name="viewport" content="width=device-width,
        initial-scale=1, shrink-to-fit=no">
        <link rel="stylesheet" href="https://stackpath.
        bootstrapcdn.com/bootstrap/4.2.1/css/bootstrap.min.
        css" integrity="sha384-GJzZqFGwb1QTTN6wy5
        9ffF1BuGJpLSa9DkKMp0DgiMDm4iYMj70gZWKYbI706tWS"
        crossorigin="anonymous">
        <script src="https://cdn.jsdelivr.net/npm/vue/dist/
        vue.js"></script>
        <style>
            .full-width{
                width: 100%;
                height: 90%;
            }
```

```
        </style>
    </head>
    <body>
        <div id="app_div">
            <custom_text></custom_text>
        </div>
        <script>
            Vue.component('custom_text', {
                template: '<fieldset class="container"><div
                class="row"> <div class="col-2">Custom
                Text</div> <div class="col-6"><input
                type="text" class="full-width" /></div> </
                div> </fieldset>'
            });
            var app = new Vue({
                el: "#app_div",
            });
        </script>
    </body>
</html>
```

Unlike previous chapters, in the above code, we can see **Vue. component** block. It defines a component.

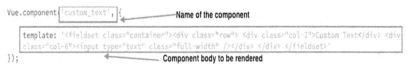

Fig 4.3: Vue component body description

As shown in the image, we can define the component name that needs to be used to render the component on screen. The component body gets defined in the template part.

We just need to use the component name as a tag to render the same on screen.

```
<custom_text></custom_text>
```

We will get the following output on screen by rendering the page in a browser.

Custom Text

Render the same component on screen; we just need to keep repeating the tags. Wherever it found the same tag inside a Vue element, it will keep rendering the controls as above.

Extend the template

It is just a text box inside a fieldset. Now, let's add another fieldset with another text box so that whenever we use the same tag, it will render two text boxes at a time.

We will make this more meaningful now. Instead of the **custom_text**, we will make it **custom_address**. Also, we will change the **Custom Text** label to **Address Line 1**.

The changes must go into the template section. So, I have appended a new fieldset with the existing one so that it will render two text boxes, one after the other.

```
<body>
    <div id="app_div">

        <custom_address></custom_address>

    </div>
    <script>
        Vue.component('custom_address', {
            template: '<fieldset class="container"><div class="row"> <div class="col-2">Address Line 1</div> <div
            class="col-8"><input type="text" class="full-width" /></div> </div> </fieldset> <fieldset
            class="container"><div class="row"> <div class="col-2">Address Line 2</div> <div class="col-8"><input
            type="text" class="full-width" /></div> </div> </fieldset>'
        });
        var app = new Vue({
            el: "#app_div",                                    Appended fieldset
        });
    </script>
</body>
```

Fig 4.4: *Adding another fieldset to the existing template*

We will render the same in the browser to see the output. Ahh.. but we ended with an error as follows:

Fig 4.5: *Error after adding the new fieldset*

It clearly states that the component template should contain exactly one root element. If we use **v-if** then we need to chain it with **v-else-**

if too, to maintain the single root. Since we have used two fieldsets one after the other, we are deviating from the rule. So, we need to add another root element to see, if that works.

Let's surround the fieldsets with a **<div>** element so that we can follow the single root element rule of Vue component.

```
template: '<div><fieldset class="container"><div class="row"> <div class="col-2">Address Line 1</div>
<div class="col-6"><input type="text" class="full-width" /></div> </div> </fieldset> <fieldset
class="container"><div class="row"> <div class="col-2">Address Line 2</div> <div class="col-6"><input
type="text" class="full-width" /></div> </div> </fieldset></div>'
```

Fig 4.6: Surround the HTML with a <div> tag

As we can see in the image above, the **<div>** element is added to the template as a single root.

Lesson learnt

Vue component template should have only one root element. We can use v-if, then we must need v-else as well to chain the elements, to keep it in one

When we use the **<custom_address></custom_address>** tag, it renders both the text boxes on screen.

Address Line 1
Address Line 2

Fig 4.7: Component output

```
<!DOCTYPE html >
<html>
    <head>
        <meta name="viewport" content="width=device-width,
        initial-scale=1, shrink-to-fit=no">

        <link rel="stylesheet" href="https://stackpath.
bootstrapcdn.com/bootstrap/4.2.1/css/bootstrap.min.css"
integrity="sha384-GJzZqFGwb1QTTN6wy59ffF1BuGJpLSa9DkKMp0Dg
iMDm4iYMj70gZWKYbI706tWS" crossorigin="anonymous">

            <script src="https://cdn.jsdelivr.net/npm/vue/
            dist/vue.js"></script>
            <style>
                .full-width{
                    width: 100%;
```

```
            height: 90%;
        }
    </style>
</head>
<body>
    <div id="app_div">
        <custom_address></custom_address>
    </div>
    <script>
        Vue.component('custom_address', {
            template: '<div><fieldset
class="container"><div class="row"> <div class="col-
2">Address Line 1</div> <div class="col-6"><input
type="text" class="full-width" /></div> </div> </
fieldset> <fieldset class="container"><div class="row">
<div class="col-2">Address Line 2</div> <div class="col-
6"><input type="text" class="full-width" /></div> </div>
</fieldset></div>'
        });
        var app = new Vue({
            el: "#app_div",
        });
    </script>
</body>
</html>
```

Dealing with data part

We have setup the text boxes. Now, we need to add value to the same. As we have seen before, in order to get the values from the text boxes, we need to have model variables assigned to the text boxes.

Let's extend the above example.

```
<script>
    Vue.component('custom_address', {
        data: function(){
            return {
                address_line1: "",
                address_line2: ""
            }
        },
        template: '<div><fieldset class="container"><div class="row"> <div class="col-2">Address Line 1</div>
        <div class="col-6"><input type="text" class="full-width" v-model="address_line1"/></div> </div>
        </fieldset> <fieldset class="container"><div class="row"> <div class="col-2">Address Line 2</div>
        <div class="col-6"><input type="text" class="full-width" v-model="address_line2"/></div> </div>
        </fieldset> </div>'
    });
    var app = new Vue({
        el: "#app_div",
    });
</script>
```

Fig 4.8: Adding data to the component

We will use two model variables here for the input texts. Model variables must be added to the data section. We will render the above example in browser.

Address Line 1
Address Line 2

We can see it is rendering correctly in the browser. Now, we need to check if the Vue component is getting value form the input boxes. In order to check the same, we need to use the Vue chrome extension.

Fig 4.9: Console view in browser to check the vue data

The strange part is no model variables here. No data is also getting populated in it. So, we need to check the console to check if there is any error in it.

Fig 4.10: Error in console window

Console tab has the error, which states that the data should be a function that returns a pre-instance value in component definitions.

We need to change the data section. It should not only contain the model variables. It should represent a function, which returns the model variable.

Since components are the reusable entities, they need to be instantiated separately to get separately rendered in screen. Each instance will have their own set of data variables. So, making the data as a function would solve the purpose. With each instance data variable would be instantiated separately.

```
<script>
    Vue.component('custom_address', {
        data: function(){
            return {
                address_line1: "",
                address_line2: ""
            }
        }
        ,
        template: '<div><fieldset class="container"><div class="row"> <div class="col-2">Address line 1</div>
        <div class="col-6"><input type="text" class="full-width" v-model="address_line1"/></div> </div>
        </fieldset> <fieldset class="container"><div class="row"> <div class="col-2">Address line 2</div>
        <div class="col-6"><input type="text" class="full-width" v-model="address_line2"/></div> </div>
        </fieldset> </div>'
    });
    var app = new Vue({
        el: "#app_div",
    });
</script>
```

Fig 4.11: Component with data in function format

Let's render the code with the instance and see how Vue component object is reacting on the screen.

Fig 4.12: vue devtool to browse the rendered Vue object

We can see the instance variable associated with the component. To see it more distinctly, let's add one more component on the screen. So that we can get to know, how data variables are behaving to the different component instances.

```
<div id="app_div">

    <custom_address></custom_address>
    <hr/>
    <custom_address></custom_address>

</div>
```

Fig 4.13: Using component in other component

We have added two components with a horizontal line. It will render on the screen accordingly.

Address Line 1
Address Line 2

Address Line 1
Address Line 2

The Vue extension tab will show the components and its model variables. Entered values in one of the component will not override the data variables in the other component.

Fig 4.14: Custom Address with data element

Fig 4.15: Another element with Custom Address with separate data element

Comparing both the image above, we can see the first component **address_line_1** has the value, how ever the same **address_line_1** in second component it has no values.

```
<!DOCTYPE html >
<html>
    <head>
        <meta name="viewport" content="width=device-width,
        initial-scale=1, shrink-to-fit=no">

        <link rel="stylesheet" href="https://stackpath.
        bootstrapcdn.com/bootstrap/4.2.1/css/bootstrap.min.
        css" integrity="sha384-GJzZqFGwb1QTTN6wy
        59ffF1BuGJpLSa9DkKMp0DgiMDm4iYMj70gZWKYbI706tWS"
        crossorigin="anonymous">

        <script src="https://cdn.jsdelivr.net/npm/vue/
        dist/vue.js"></script>
```

```
    <style>
        .full-width{
            width: 100%;
            height: 90%;
        }
    </style>
</head>
<body>
    <div id="app_div">
        <custom_address></custom_address>
        <hr/>
        <custom_address></custom_address>
    </div>
    <script>
        Vue.component('custom_address', {
            data: function(){
                return {
                    address_line1: "",
                    address_line2: ""
                }
            }
            ,
            template: '<div><fieldset
            class="container"><div class="row">
            <div class="col-2">Address Line 1</div>
            <div class="col-6"><input type="text"
            class="full-width" v-model="address_
            line1"/></div> </div> </fieldset> <fieldset
            class="container"><div class="row">
            <div class="col-2">Address Line 2</div>
            <div class="col-6"><input type="text"
            class="full-width" v-model="address_
            line2"/></div> </div> </fieldset> </div>'
        });
        var app = new Vue({
            el: "#app_div",
        });
    </script>
</body>
</html>
```

Template string looks odd !!!

The template string looks very odd. Think of a template with multiple text boxes, drop downs, check boxes and buttons. Putting them in string would not be an issue. The issue arises when the maintenance phase comes in. It would be very high cost to maintain the application. We may need to use some kind of external tool or something in order to understand the template string.

So, now we should think of something else, which will be help for us to write the template string in a better and organized way so that we can maintain the same efficiency in future. Vue CLI is the answer for the same.

Let's create a new component using CLI. We will analyze different part of it in the following sections.

To setup and run the Vue CLI, please refer to day 1.

So, we will now create a new CLI project and add components to it. Let's do this in a step wise manner.

$ Vue create learnin7days

$ cd learnin7days

$ npm run serve

As per the above command, we have setup the project, navigated into the directory and run the server. We will get the following output:

```
DONE  Compiled successfully in 6321ms


App running at:
 - Local:    http://localhost:8081/
 - Network:  http://192.168.43.111:8081/

Note that the development build is not optimized.
To create a production build, run npm run build.
```

Fig 4.16: Server ran successfully

We can see the output in a web browser using the links specified above **http://localhost:8081**. If we look into the folder structure of the newly created project. We will use **.vue** files. There are the files which contain the component code.

Fig 4.17: Vue CLI project

The generated **HelloWorld.vue** component contains the code which can be maintained easily. If we look into it, we will realize the template is no more a string here.

```
 1  <template>
 2    <div class="hello">
 3      <h1>{{ msg }}</h1>
 4      <p>
 5        For a guide and recipes on how to configure / customize this project,<br>
 6        check out the
 7        <a href="https://cli.vuejs.org" target="_blank" rel="noopener">vue-cli documentation</a>.
 8      </p>
 9      <h3>Installed CLI Plugins</h3>
10      <ul>
11        <li><a href="https://github.com/vuejs/vue-cli/tree/dev/packages/%40vue/cli-plugin-babel" target="_blank"
           rel="noopener">babel</a></li>
12        <li><a href="https://github.com/vuejs/vue-cli/tree/dev/packages/%40vue/cli-plugin-eslint" target="_blank"
           rel="noopener">eslint</a></li>
13      </ul>
14      <h3>Essential Links</h3>
15      <ul>
16        <li><a href="https://vuejs.org" target="_blank" rel="noopener">Core Docs</a></li>
17        <li><a href="https://forum.vuejs.org" target="_blank" rel="noopener">Forum</a></li>
18        <li><a href="https://chat.vuejs.org" target="_blank" rel="noopener">Community Chat</a></li>
19        <li><a href="https://twitter.com/vuejs" target="_blank" rel="noopener">Twitter</a></li>
20        <li><a href="https://news.vuejs.org" target="_blank" rel="noopener">News</a></li>
21      </ul>
22      <h3>Ecosystem</h3>
23      <ul>
24        <li><a href="https://router.vuejs.org" target="_blank" rel="noopener">vue-router</a></li>
25        <li><a href="https://vuex.vuejs.org" target="_blank" rel="noopener">vuex</a></li>
26        <li><a href="https://github.com/vuejs/vue-devtools#vue-devtools" target="_blank" rel="noopener">vue-
           devtools</a></li>
27        <li><a href="https://vue-loader.vuejs.org" target="_blank" rel="noopener">vue-loader</a></li>
28        <li><a href="https://github.com/vuejs/awesome-vue" target="_blank" rel="noopener">awesome-vue</a></li>
29      </ul>
30    </div>
31  </template>
32
33  <script>
34  export default {
35    name: 'HelloWorld',
36    props: {
37      msg: String
38    }
39  }
40  </script>
41
```

Fig 4.18: Default created component code with template

Editor/IDE, such as brackets **(http://brackets.io/)**, VS Code**(https://code.visualstudio.com/)**, sublime **(https://www.sublimetext.com/)** and so on. can be used to open and edit the project. The editor list is very long; it is not limited to the above. You can find any of your comfortable editors to work with. We will create the same address component using the vue CLI.

As we have seen previously, the **.vue** file i.e. the component files all stored in /**components** folder. So we will add a new file named as **Address.vue** to the /**components** folder. Then let's add the following code into that file.

The code contains the template string in **<templates>** tag. Name of the component can be defined inside the **<script>** tag. Like other web pages, we can have a style property to styling the template when it gets render.

```
<template>
    <div>
        <fieldset class="container">
            <div class="row">
                <div class="col-2">Address Line 1</div>
                <div class="col-6">
                    <input type="text" class="full-width"
                    v-model="address_line1"/>
                </div>
            </div>
        </fieldset>
        <fieldset class="container">
            <div class="row">
                <div class="col-2">Address Line 2</div>
                <div class="col-6">
                    <input type="text" class="full-width"
                    v-model="address_line2"/>
                </div>
            </div>
        </fieldset>
    </div>
</template>

<script>
    export default {
        name: 'Address',
        data: function(){
            return {
                address_line1: "",
```

```
                    address_line2: ""
                }
            }
        }
</script>

<style scoped>

.full-width{
    width: 100%;
    height: 90%;
}

</style>
```

Job is not done yet !!

Now we need to put this **Address.vue** link into the **app.vue** so that it will be rendered in screen. In **App.vue**, we will refer this component so that the same components get found and initialized in the main view.

Now let's make changes to the **App.vue.** We will refer the Address component in the **App.vue.**

```
<template>
  <div id="app">
    <img alt="Vue logo" src="./assets/logo.png">
    <Address></Address>
  </div>
</template>

<script>
import Address from './components/Address.vue'

export default {
  name: 'app',
  components: {
   Address
  }
}
</script>

<style>
#app {
  font-family: 'Avenir', Helvetica, Arial, sans-serif;
```

```
-webkit-font-smoothing: antialiased;
-moz-osx-font-smoothing: grayscale;
text-align: center;
color: #2c3e50;
margin-top: 60px;
max-width: 40%
}
</style>
```

As shown in the code, we have registered the component and used the same. Like we have demonstrated the same in one of our examples previously.

Fig 4.19: Browser screenshot of the component designed in Vue CLI

Passing properties to the components

We can reuse the components, but it needs some input from outside in order to reflect the same on screen. Let's look at the following image:

First Addresses

    Address Line 1
    Address Line 2

Second Address

    Address Line 1
    Address Line 2

Fig 4.20: Expected output, same component with different caption

It is using the component we have built in our last example and rendering the controls in two instances. Apart from that, we have two personalize labels i.e. **First Address** and **Second Address**. How is that possible?

The magic is done by props. We need to define the properties in the component to accept the data from outside.

```
<script>
    Vue.component('custom_address', {
        props: ['title'],
        data: function(){
            return {
                address_line1: "",
                address_line2: ""
            }
        }
        template: '<div>{{ title }}<fieldset class="container"><div class="row"> <div class="col-2">Address
        line 1</div> <div class="col-6"><input type="text" class="full-width" v-model="address_line1"/></div
        </div> </fieldset> <fieldset class="container"><div class="row"> <div class="col-2">Address line
        2</div> <div class="col-6"><input type="text" class="full-width" v-model="address_line2"/></div>
        </div> </fieldset> </div>'
    });
    var app = new Vue({
        el: "#app_div",
    });
</script>
```

Fig 4.21: Demonstrating Props in the component

Props take the array of properties and it gets received in the component. We have made that property visible in the template with a string interpolation {{ **title** }}.

In the HTML, we need to pass the property into the component tag.

```
<custom_address title="First Addresses"></custom_address>
<hr/>
<custom_address  title="Second Address"></custom_address>
```

Fig 4.22: Passing props in the tag

The text passed using the title property in the HTML tag, gets captured by the title property in the component. As mentioned in the template the title attribute gets displayed on the screen.

Registering the components

To use a component in the Vue application, we need to register the same. So that the application knows it and renders the same on screen.

Registration is of two types:

- **Local registration:** Registering the component in a local scope where it will get used. Mostly needed when a single component is being used in one or few components. It makes perfect sense to get it registered in the local scope of those components only.

- **Global registration:** Registering the component in project level scope. It is needed when the component gets used in multiple places/components in a project scope. It should be accessible through out project.

Registering a component locally

We will extend the **Address** component, which we have created recently, with a user component. In that address component, we will show a fixed list of users in a dropdown.

Let's add a new component to our existing **Day4/learnin7days** project and name it as **User**. The file in the /**components** would be **User.vue**.

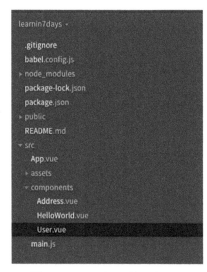

Fig 4.23: *File structure after adding User component*

In this user component, we will add the template code to in **user.vue** to render a dropdown. A fixed array of users will be passed to the component. The same array elements will get rendered in the dropdown.

```
<template>
    <select class="full-width">
        <option v-for="user in users">{{ user }} </option>
    </select>
</template>

<script>
export default {
  name: 'Users',
  data: function(){
      return {
          users: ['Dr. Vishal Jain', 'Nirmal Hota',
```

```
'Tadit Dash']
        }
    }


}
</script>

<style scoped>
    .full-width{
        width: 100%;
        height: 41px;
        font-size: larger;
    }
</style>
```

As mentioned earlier, the list must be rendered with the address component. So, we need to register the user component with the address.

```
<script>
import User from './User.vue'

export default {
  name: 'Address',
  data: function(){
        return {
            address_line1: "",
            address_line2: ""
        }
    },
  components: {
    User
  }
}
</script>
```

Fig 4.24: User component registered within the Address component

To register the component, we need to import the same into the scope. As we can see in the above image, we have imported the user component into the address component. Then we have declared the user component under the components section of the address component. Now, we can include the **<User>** tag in the template section of the address component so that it will render on screen, as if it is a part of the same component.

Fig 4.25: *Browser screenshot : User component showing with address component*

In the screenshot above the shown dropdown is the user component, which got rendered with the address component. Let's see the following Address component code.

```
<template>
    <div>
        <fieldset class="container">
            <div class="row">
                <div class="col-2">Address Line 1</div>
                <div class="col-6">
                    <input type="text" class="full-width"
                    v-model="address_line1"/>
                </div>
            </div>
        </fieldset>
        <fieldset class="container">
            <div class="row">
                <div class="col-2">Address Line 2</div>
                <div class="col-6">
                    <input type="text" class="full-width"
                    v-model="address_line2"/>
                </div>
            </div>
        </fieldset>
        <User></User>
    </div>
</template>
<script>
```

```
import User from './User.vue'
export default {
  name: 'Address',
  data: function(){
      return {
          address_line1: "",
          address_line2: ""
      }
  },
  components: {
    User
  }
}
</script>
<style scoped>

.full-width{
    width: 100%;
    height: 90%;
}
</style>
```

Are you sure it won't get access globally?

To answer this question let's try to use the **<User></User>** component tag in the **App.vue** page. **App.vue** page is the root component, which gets rendered in the **public/index.html.** So, to try the same, let's replace the **<Address></Address>** with **<User></User>**.

Fig 4.26: Browser console error while accessing User component globally

The screen rendered blank and we can see the error in the console, which says the *Unknown custom element: <User> - did you register the component correctly? .....* This statement gives us the clue that the component is not accessible in **App.vue** component as it is registered locally in the **Address.vue** component.

Let's do a global registration and check if the **App.vue** can render the same component on screen.

Global registration of a component

As discussed earlier, global registration is only useful, if we use the component in multiple places of the project. Otherwise the local registration is advisable.

We will use the above **User** component and register the same globally so that it can be accessed in any page of our project. **Main.js** is the file which is accessible globally. So, we need to import our component in that file and initialize the same in that.

```
import Vue from 'vue'
import App from './App.vue'
import User from './components/User.vue'
Vue.config.productionTip = false
Vue.component('User', User)
new Vue({
  render: h => h(App)
}).$mount('#app')
```

Vue.component is the way we normally define the component. Here too we did the same. Then we have added a component name '**User**' to the newly created component. Finally, points that component to the **User** component object.

Now, we can access the same **<User></User>** component from any of the pages. It will render the user dropdown.

Organizing the components

As we have discussed earlier, components are the reusable entities. They need to be created as if those can be reused in multiple places. Depending upon the usability, the component registration can be done accordingly.

Fig 4.27: Organizing components
(Pic courtesy: https://vuejs.org/v2/guide/components.html)

As we can see in the tree representation, the nesting of component should be done as per the need and places of use of the component.

Data passing between components

We can nest components as and when needed. It is really needed to pass data from parent component to the child component in the tree. We will use the props to send the data between the parent child components.

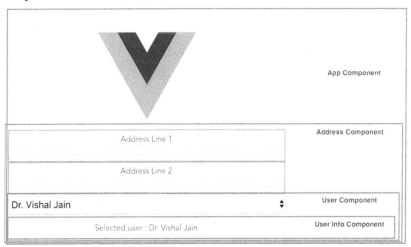

Fig 4.28: Demonstration of component placement on screen

As we can see in the image, the **App** is the main component for us. We have nested the **Address** component inside the **App** component then **User** component in the address component. Similarly, **User Info** component in **User** component.

We can also see the user dropdown change reflects in the **UserInfo** component. Since they are two different components, then the data passing between them is really happening. This data passing is done with the props.

```
<template>
    <p>Selected user : {{ usrInfo }}</p>
</template>
<script>
export default {
  name: 'UserInfo',
  props: [
    'usrInfo'
  ],
}
</script>
```

In this **Userinfo** component, we are having a **<p>** tag to display the selected user on screen. This **<p>** tag is fetching its data from the **usrInfo** props.

Now we can check the **User** component to see how the data is getting passed to the **UserInfo**, which is the child component here.

```
<template>
    <div>
        <select class="full-width" v-model='selectedUser'>
            <option v-for="user in users" :key="user"> {{ user }} </option>
        </select>
        <UserInfo :usrInfo = 'selectedUser'></UserInfo>
    </div>
</template>
```

Fig 4.29: *Showing the usage of UserInfo child component*

In the template, it is using the **UserInfo** tag and passed the value in the **usrInfo** property, which we have defined in the **UserInfo** component. So that **UserInfo** component would get the data from the property and displays the data in the **<p>** tag. The full base of the **User** component would look like the following:

```
<template>
    <div>
        <select class="full-width" v-model='selectedUser'>
            <option v-for="user in users" :key="user"> {{
            user }} </option>
        </select>
        <UserInfo :usrInfo = 'selectedUser'></UserInfo>
```

```
    </div>
</template>
<script>
import UserInfo from './UserInfo.vue'

 export default {
   name: 'Users',
   data: function(){
       return {
            users: ['Dr. Vishal Jain', 'Nirmal Hota',
            'Tadit Dash'],
            selectedUser: ''
        }
   },
   components: {
     UserInfo
   }
}
</script>

<style scoped>
    .full-width{
        width: 100%;
        height: 41px;
        font-size: larger;
    }
</style>
```

Handle child component event in parent

Till now, we can see how the data is being passed from child component to the parent component and vice versa. But the data passing is not the end of the story. In a real world we must need to handle the child events in the parent too.

To pass the event from child to parent, we need to use the defined key word **$emit**. As the name suggests, it emits the event from child to parent. Parent must handle the event in its end to mark the effect.

Let's create another vue component and name it as **AddressWithPinCheck**.vue. We will add the pin code input here, so that it will accept the pin code from the user. In addition to that, we will add a button. On click of the button, it will validate the pin code.

```
<fieldset class="container">
    <div class="row">
        <div class="col-2">Pin Code</div>
        <div class="col-6">
            <input type="text" class="full-width" v-model="pin_code"/>
            <button v-on:click= "$emit('validate_pin', pin_code)">Validate</button>
        </div>
    </div>
</fieldset>
```

Fig 4.30: Using $emit to validate pincode

Everything looks familiar to us, apart from **"$emit('validate_pin', pin_code)"** statement. This statement emits the **validate_pin** event to parent. Now, parent has to handle the event in order to get the desired result.

In this case, this component emits the **validate_pin** and the parent will implement to show the message.

```
<template>
  <div id="app">
    <img alt="Vue logo" src="./assets/logo.png">
    <AddressWithPinCheck v-on:validate_pin="validate_
    pin"></AddressWithPinCheck>
  </div>
</template>

<script>
import AddressWithPinCheck from './components/
AddressWithPinCheck.vue'

export default {
  name: 'app',
  components: {
   AddressWithPinCheck,
  },
  methods: {
    validate_pin: function(pinCode){
        var pat1=/^\d{6}$/;
        if(pinCode!=""){
            if(pat1.test(pinCode)){
                alert(pinCode + " is a valid pincode.");
            }
            else{
                alert(pinCode + " is invalid. Please check
                again.");
            }
```

```
        }
        else{
            alert("Pincode should not be blank");
        }
    }
  }
}
</script>

<style>
#app {
  font-family: 'Avenir', Helvetica, Arial, sans-serif;
  -webkit-font-smoothing: antialiased;
  -moz-osx-font-smoothing: grayscale;
  text-align: center;
  color: #2c3e50;
  margin-top: 60px;
  max-width: 40%
}
</style>
```

In the above code, we have noticed two things. One is, the way component tag is used and the other one is how the event is handled.

```
<AddressWithPinCheck v-on:validate_pin="validate_pin"></
AddressWithPinCheck>
```

In this statement, we are using the component and along with the component user is handling the event emitted by the component. **validate_pin** is the event emitted by the component, which is in v-on. To make this event worked, we have defined a custom method **validate_pin**. This event name must not be same as the event name. We can take any custom name.

We have learned the basics of a component. The reusability is the key to use the component. It helps us to reduce the writing of same code repeatedly. We can define properties of components to accept data from the page as well as parent component. We also learnt, how the validation and type can be mentioned for the properties. So that properties get the valid values as per the spec defined. Also, the string template is better to replace with the .vue files, which would help in

writing better managed HTML codes. Event can be handled in parent which is emitted from children and data can be passed through it. $emit is the key to expose event from child to parent.

In the next chapter, we will learn how to work more with the components. We will also learn how to establish the communication back from child component to the parent components. We will see how we can create and use the custom events. We will also learn the dynamic components, async components, and so on. In this chapter, we will also cover the slot and how useful they are.

DAY 5

Components in Depth

In the previous chapter, we learnt the way to create the components. Reusability and maintainability is the key to use the components. It helps us segregating our work in multiple small pieces. We also explored the way to use components in another component. The passing mechanism also helped us to pass data between the components.

In this chapter, we will dive deep into the components. We will visit deeper with the props. We will define the types, apply validations, and so on. Also, we will play more with the components and learn how slot is going to help us.

Diving in the props

As we have discussed in our previous chapter, props are the ways to pass the data to and from the components. It helps data communication between the parent and children components.

In this chapter, we will look more into the implementation of the prop validations.

Props type validation

We can apply the validation on the props while defining them. The child component has the full rights to decide what to accept and what not. So, prop block can specify the type of the property.

Let's create a vue component, which will accept the numeric values only. Also, we can mark it as required. So that whenever the component tag gets used, it will be needing the property value.

```
<template>
  <p>Number is {{ NumValue}}</p>
</template>

<script>
export default {
  name: 'NumberBoard',
  props: {
   NumValue: {
        type: Number
    }
  },
}
</script>
```

We have defined a property called **NumValue** and specified the type of value it accepts. In order to check, how it works, we need to pass the value into the component.

```
 <template>
  <div id="app">
    <img alt="Vue logo" src="./assets/logo.png">
    <NumberBoard NumValue="11"></NumberBoard>
  </div>
</template>
<script>
import NumberBoard from './components/NumberBoard.vue'
export default {
  name: 'app',
  components: {
   NumberBoard
  }
}
</script>
```

We have passed the number value into the component and it is rendering correctly on the screen.

Fig 5.1: Displaying the numeric value passed to prop

We can do a little experiment by adding the string value instead of the number. Let's add a string instead of a number in the **NumValue** prop of the **<NumberBoard>** tag.

```
<template>
  <div id="app">
    <img alt="Vue logo" src="./assets/logo.png">
    <NumberBoard NumValue="This is not a number"></NumberBoard>
  </div>
</template>

<script>
import NumberBoard from './components/NumberBoard.vue'

export default {
  name: 'app',
  components: {
   NumberBoard
  }
}
</script>
```

If we switch back to the browser screen, although it is rendered on screen but there must be an error in console. Now, let's notice the console in dev tools. The console clearly displays the error there.

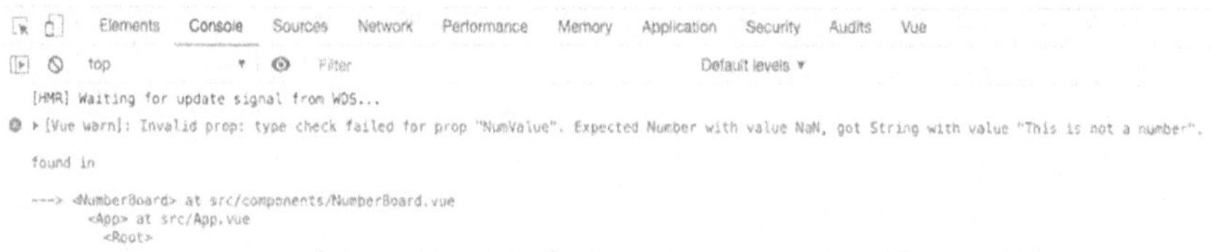

Fig 5.2: Error when non-numeric values passed

The error clearly says that the value is invalid. So, we can conclude from the above experiment that the values get accepted as per the type defined. It gets resolved, if we change the prop value from String to Number.

The default value for the prop is Any. Not setting any type OR setting the type to null would accept the any type of data.

Supported types in a property are:

String	Accepts the string value
Number	Accepts the numbers
Boolean	Accepts true / false values
Object	Accepts an object
Array	Array can be passed into the property
Function	It can accept a function code block as well
Date	Accepts date
Symbol	Accepts symbols

Passing an Array to property

Like String, Number, and Boolean we can also pass arrays to the properties. We will pass a static array to the component and iterate through it to print the elements on screen.

Although, we pass static array but we will use v-bind. So that browser treats it is as JavaScript expression than a string.

```
<template>
    <ul>
        <li v-for="alphabet in alphabets"
v-bind:key='alphabet'>{{ alphabet }}</li>
    </ul>
</template>
```

```
<script>
export default {
  name: 'Alphabets',
  props: {
    alphabets: {
        type: Array
    }
  },
}
</script>
```

In this component code snippet, we can see the alphabets prop. We are using the type here as the Array. We will iterate in the same array to display the array element in the <li> tag.

The following code snippet demonstrate how we can create the array and pass the same to the component property:

```
<template>
  <div id="app">
    <img alt="Vue logo" src="./assets/logo.png">
    <Alphabets v-bind:alphabets="['A', 'B', 'C', 'D']"></
    Alphabets>
  </div>
</template>
<script>
import Alphabets from './components/Alphabets.vue'
export default {
  name: 'app',
  components: {
      Alphabets
  }
}
</script>
```

Passing Object to property

We can also pass objects to the properties. We have seen in this chapter, we can pass string, number, Boolean and arrays. We can also pass the object into the property so that they can be processed by the component.

```
<template>
    <div>
```

```
            <p><b>Country : {{ countryDetails.name }} </b></p>
            <p>Capital City : {{ countryDetails.capital_name
            }}</p>
            <p>Population : {{ countryDetails.population }}</p>
            <p>Dialing code : {{ countryDetails.dialing_code
            }}</p>
        </div>
</template>

<script>
export default {
  name: 'CountryDetails',
  props: {
    countryDetails: {
        type: Object
    }
  },
}
</script>
```

As shown in the above code snippet, we have mentioned the type of the prop as **Object**. So, whenever we consume the properties, we need to pass the object type value.

```
<template>
  <div id="app">
    <img alt="Vue logo" src="./assets/logo.png">
    <CountryDetails v-bind:countryDetails="{name: 'India',
    capital_name: 'New Delhi', population: 'More than 133
    Crores', dialing_code: '91' }"></CountryDetails>
  </div>
</template>

<script>
import CountryDetails from './components/CountryDetails.vue'

export default {
  name: 'app',
  components: {
   CountryDetails
  }
}
</script>
```

We have created a JSON object containing the attributes and passed into the property. The component is implemented in a way to extract the values from the object and print that on screen.

Property with multiple types

One property can be of multiple types as well. Let's take an example property. Set **String** and **Number** as type assignments to it.

```
<template>
    <p>My Value is : {{ MyValue }}</p>
</template>

<script>
export default {
  name: 'MultiType',
  props: {
    MyValue: {
        type: [Number, String]
    }
  },
}
</script>
```

Now, let's validate three use cases here. First, we will assign a Number and check, if any error. We will check in the inspect window console. No errors! working fine.

```
<template>
  <div id="app">
    <img alt="Vue logo" src="./assets/logo.png">
    <MultiTypeValidation :MyValue="5"></
MultiTypeValidation>
  </div>
</template>

<script>
import MultiTypeValidation from './components/
MultiTypeValidation.vue'

export default {
  name: 'app',
  components: {
   MultiTypeValidation
  }
```

```
}
</script>
```

Now, let's assign a string value to ensure it is causing no errors in the console.

```
<template>
  <div id="app">
    <img alt="Vue logo" src="./assets/logo.png">
    <MultiTypeValidation MyValue="Life is beautiful"></
MultiTypeValidation>
  </div>
</template>

<script>
import MultiTypeValidation from './components/
MultiTypeValidation.vue'

export default {
  name: 'app',
  components: {
   MultiTypeValidation
   }
}
</script>
```

So, all the above works fine without any error. Let's check if really the multi type works? We will assign an object now. Then we will watch out the console to see, if any error.

```
<template>
  <div id="app">
    <img alt="Vue logo" src="./assets/logo.png">
    <MultiTypeValidation v-bind:MyValue="{name: 'India',
capital_name: 'New Delhi'}"></MultiTypeValidation>
  </div>
</template>

<script>
import MultiTypeValidation from './components/
MultiTypeValidation.vue'

export default {
  name: 'app',
  components: {
   MultiTypeValidation
```

```
    }
}
</script>
```

Although we can see the output on screen, let's check the console window. It has the warning there.

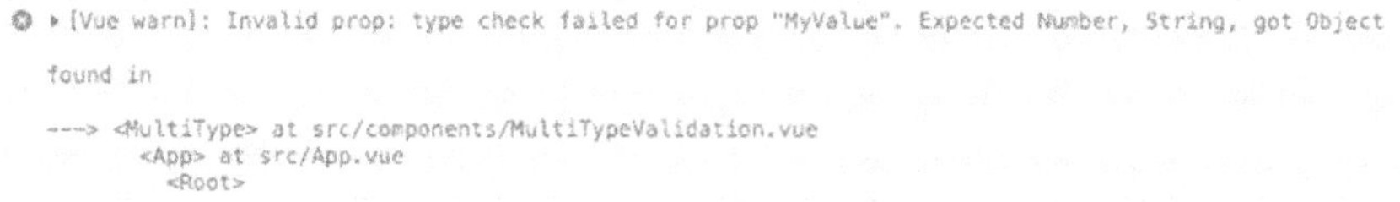

```
⚠ ▶ [Vue warn]: Invalid prop: type check failed for prop "MyValue". Expected Number, String, got Object
    found in
    ---> <MultiType> at src/components/MultiTypeValidation.vue
            <App> at src/App.vue
                <Root>
```

Fig 5.3: Browser console error showing the prop type check failed

The warning clearly says, it expects the **Number** or **String** but, got an object.

Making the property mandatory

To make the property mandatory with the component, we can add an additional attribute called **required**.

```
<template>
    <p>Number is {{ NumValue }}</p>
</template>

<script>
export default {
  name: 'NumberBoard',
  props: {
    NumValue: {
        type: Number,
        required: true
    }
  },
}
</script>
```

Now we have marked the **NumValue** as required. We will instantiate the component in the HTML without the **NumValue** property.

```
<template>
  <div id="app">
    <img alt="Vue logo" src="./assets/logo.png">
    <NumberBoard></NumberBoard>
  </div>
```

```
</template>

<script>
 import NumberBoard from './components/NumberBoard.vue'

export default {
   name: 'app',
   components: {
     NumberBoard
   }
}
</script>
```

We have used the **<NumberBoard>** tag without the **NumValue** property. Let's check the console.

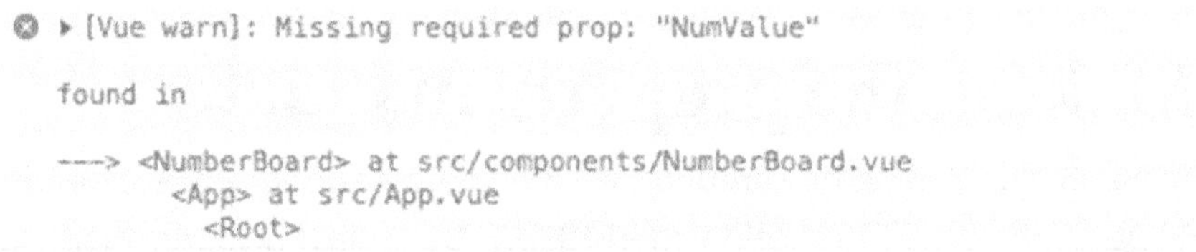

```
⊗ ▸ [Vue warn]: Missing required prop: "NumValue"

   found in

   ---> <NumberBoard> at src/components/NumberBoard.vue
          <App> at src/App.vue
            <Root>
```

Fig 5.4: Displaying error for missing prop value

The prop missing warning is there in the console. It indicates, if the *"required"* param is set to *"true"*, then it will look for the prop as and when the component gets instantiated.

Custom validation in property

Apart from the fixed type validations, we can also add custom validators to the props. We can do that using the *"validator"* level in the prop. It accepts the custom defined function, which can validate the prop values.

```
<template>
    <p>My Value is : {{ MyValue }}</p>
</template>

<script>
export default {
   name: 'MultiType',
   props: {
     MyValue: {
         type: Number,
         validator: value => {
```

```
        return value > 0;
      }
    }
  },
}
</script>
```

In this validator, we have added a function which checks if the number value is greater than 0.

```
<template>
  <div id="app">
    <img alt="Vue logo" src="./assets/logo.png">
    <CustomValidation :MyValue="-1"></CustomValidation>
  </div>
</template>

<script>
import CustomValidation from './components/
CustomValidation.vue'

export default {
  name: 'app',
  components: {
   CustomValidation
  }
}
</script>
```

Let's test the validator. So we have added -1 to the prop, as shown in the above snippet. We need to check the console window in order to see, if the validator works. Yes, we saw the warning message here in the console.

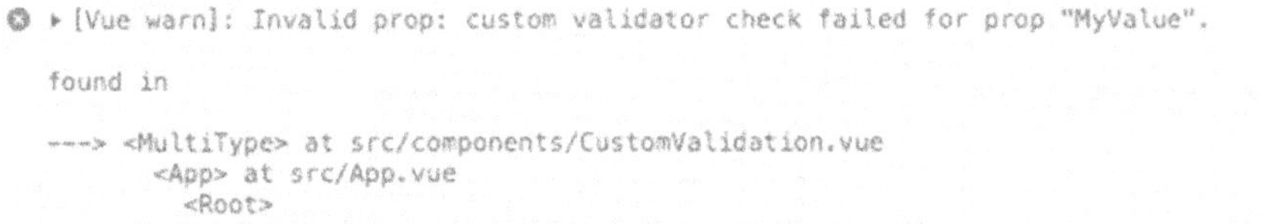

```
⊗ ▸ [Vue warn]: Invalid prop: custom validator check failed for prop "MyValue".

  found in

  ---> <MultiType> at src/components/CustomValidation.vue
         <App> at src/App.vue
           <Root>
```

Fig 5.5: Console error for failed custom validator

Default value in property

We can also assign a default value to the property as well, so that in the absence of a value, it works like a value being received.

```
<template>
  <p>Number is {{ NumValue}}</p>
</template>

<script>
export default {
  name: 'NumberBoard',
  props: {
   NumValue: {
        type: Number,
      required: true,
        default: 123
    }
  },
}
</script>
```

In absence of the input value, the default value fills the gap. The default value gets used by the component.

Slots

Slots are way to inject the parent component contents into the child components. We may argue that, we can use the props for the same, but think of a textual content of some lines, and so on. They are not the feasible ones to be shared using props.

Using Slot

To use slot mechanism, we need to use the **<slot> </slot>** tag. This tag enables vue to inject the parent component contents into the child component.

Use Slot to inject content

Let's create a new vue component with the **<slot>** tag. We will use the vue component in our parent component to check how it works. Let's name the component as the **BasicSlot**. Vue along with the following code added to it.

```
<template>
  <div>
    <p>This is the child componet which we will use to
    demonstrate the slot way of working. </p>
```

```
    <slot></slot>
  </div>
</template>
```

As shown in the code, we have added the **<slot></slot>** tag along with the other contents in the child component.

Now let's import the component in the parent component, and add some content into it to check how **<slot>** is working.

```
<template>
  <div id="app">
    <img alt="Vue logo" src="./assets/logo.png">
    <BasicSlot>
      <p>Now, we can see the injected content from the
      parent.</p>
      <p>It is very easy.</p>
    </BasicSlot>
  </div>
</template>

<script>
import BasicSlot from './components/Slots/BasicSlot.vue'
export default {
  name: 'app',
  components: {
   BasicSlot
  }
}
</script>
```

As shown in the preceding code, we have added text content into the **<BasicSlot>** component in the parent component.

It will inject the content specified in the parent component into the child component **<slot>** tag along with the content of the child component as we can see in the following image which clearly indicate the contents. The top rectangle indicates the child component content, and the bottom rectangle indicates the parent component contents.

Child Component Content

This is the child componet which we will use to demonstrate the slot way of working.

Now, we can see the injected content from the parent.

It is very easy.   **Parent Component Content**

Fig 5.6: Displaying the slot content for both child and parent

Incase we want to display the same parent content multiple times, then we need to add the **<slot></slot>** tag in it multiple times too. In other words, Vue keeps injecting the content in the child component as many times the **<slot>** tag is found.

Fallback Content

Parent content gets injected into the child component. So what if, the child has some content in there? Will it replace the content? That's right.

If the child has some content in the slot and parent has also some content, then the child content gets overridden by the parent content. But if the parent content is empty, then the child content will be shown on screen.

```
<template>
  <div>
    <p>
        <slot>
            <p>The parent content is blank. So it is
            showing the child content.</p>
        </slot>
    </p>
  </div>
</template>
```

Let's add a new component with the **<slot>** tag implemented. We have added a line of text to know, if the parent component content overrides the child one. We will use the same component in a parent component and pass the content inside the tag.

```
<template>
  <div id="app">
    <img alt="Vue logo" src="./assets/logo.png">
    <OverideSlot>
      This is the parent content. It has overriden the child
      content.
    </OverideSlot>
  </div>
</template>

<script>
import OverideSlot from './components/Slots/OverideSlot.
vue'
export default {
  name: 'app,
  components: {
   OverideSlot
  }
}
</script>
```

We have used the **<OverideSlot>** tag in the parent and passed the text in it. In the browser, we can see, as shown in the following screenshot, the parent content is getting displayed by overriding the child content.

This is the parent content. It has overriden the child content.

Fig 5.7: Displaying parent content by overriding the child content

We will enhance the same example, by removing the parent content. As a result, it should render the child content in the browser.

```
<template>
  <div id="app">
    <img alt="Vue logo" src="./assets/logo.png">
    <OverideSlot></OverideSlot>
  </div>
</template>

<script>

import OverideSlot from './components/Slots/OverideSlot.
vue'
export default {
  name: 'app',
  components: {
   OverideSlot
  }
}
</script>
```

This is the parent content. It has overriden the child content.

Fig 5.8: *Displaying parent content, when child content is empty*

Named Slot

Till now, we learnt to replace the parent content in the child component. But they seem really uncontrollable. It will get replaced as and when they get the **<slot>** tag. But we must need a controlled replacement.

Named slots are usually being used when the parent components are meant to be replaced in certain places in the child components.

```
<template>
  <div>
        <slot name="header-slot"></slot>
    <div>
        <slot>
        </slot>
    </div>
    <slot name="footer-slot"></slot>
  </div>
</template>
```

We have created the component with three slots. Header and footer are the two named slots defined in the template. The slot in the middle will get replaced without the name.

```
<template>
  <div id="app">
    <img alt="Vue logo" src="./assets/logo.png">
    <NamedSlot>
        <template v-slot:header-slot>
            <div style="padding-bottom: 20px">
              <p style="font-weight: bold; font-size: 120%">
                    Welcome to the Named Slot Lession
              </p>
            </div>
        </template>
```

Named slots are very helpful in the real life development scenarios. It gives the control over the content injection from parent to the child.

```
        <template v-slot:footer-slot>
            <div style="padding-top: 20px">
              <p style="font-weight: bold; font-size: 80%">
                    Thanks for reading
              </p>
            </div>
        </template>
    </NamedSlot>
  </div>
</template>

<script>
import NamedSlot from './components/Slots/NamedSlot.vue'
```

```
export default {
  name: 'app',
  components: {
   NamedSlot
  }
}
</script>
```

Welcome to the Named Slot Lession

Named slots are very helpful in the real life development scenarios. It gives the
control over the content injection from parent to the child.

Thanks for reading

Fig 5.9: Rendering named slot

The header slot rendered on top and the footer slot is at footer, with the content in the middle, which is not a named slot.

The named slot content should be wrapped inside the **<template>** tag with the **v-slot** attribute. Contents without the **<template>** tag will get rendered in the **<slot>** tag. They can also be placed in a **v-slot** template as shown in the following:

```
<template v-slot:default>
    Named slots are very helpful in the real-life
    development scenarios. It gives the control
    over the content injection from parent to the
    child.
</template>
```

Scoped Slot

Sometimes we may need to deal with the situations, where the objects need to be passed from child to parent to inject the slot content.

Let's take an example, where the parent slot needs to inject a country capital into the slot content of the child. This is quite easy, if the country object is present in the parent. But if the object is in the child end, and we need to push the content from the parent.

```
<slot v-bind:country="country">
</slot>
```

We need to use the **v-bind** technique here to send the object from child to parent component.

```
<template>
  <div>
        <slot v-bind:country="country">
        </slot>
  </div>
</template>
<script>
export default {
  name: 'app',
  data(){
    return {
        country: {name: 'India', capital: 'New Delhi'}
    }
  },
}
</script>
```

The country object is bound to the slot with **v-bind**. This is called **Slot Props**. Slot props can now be accessed in the parent end along with same values.

```
<template>
  <div id="app">
    <img alt="Vue logo" src="./assets/logo.png">
    <ScopedSlot v-slot:default="childslotprop">
        {{ childslotprop.country.capital }}
    </ScopedSlot>

  </div>
</template>

<script>
import ScopedSlot from './components/Slots/ScopedSlot.vue'
export default {
```

```
name: 'app',
components: {
 ScopedSlot
 }
}
</script>
```

We have used the slot prop attribute to receive the country object from the child. We can use any variable as the slot prop to receive the slot object.

If the value from parent needs to be pushed into only one slot, then we may follow the abbreviated approach as follows.

```
<ScopedSlot v-slot="childslotprop">
    {{ childslotprop.country.capital }}|
</ScopedSlot>
```

Consider there are multiple slots that need the value to be pushed, we may also follow the template approach.

```
<template>
  <div>
    <slot name="header-slot"></slot>
    <div>
        <slot v-bind:country="country">
        </slot>
    </div>
    <slot name="footer-slot"></slot>
  </div>
</template>
<script>
export default {
  name: 'app',
  data(){
    return {
        country: {name: 'India', capital: 'New Delhi'}
    }
  },
}
</script>
```

We have defined two named slot and a default slot to get the content from the parent. In the default slot, we have passed the country object using **v-bind**.

Parent will push the content into the header and footer slots using the named slots and the default slot will get the values using the slot props.

```
<ScopedSlot>
        <template v-slot:header-slot>
            <div style="padding-bottom: 20px">
              <p style="font-weight: bold; font-size: 120%">
                   Welcome to the Country Object
              </p>
            </div>
        </template>

        <template v-slot:default="childslotprop">
            {{ childslotprop.country.capital }}
        </template>

        <template v-slot:footer-slot>
            <div style="padding-top: 20px">
              <p style="font-weight: bold; font-size: 80%">
                   Thanks for reading
              </p>
            </div>
        </template>

    </ScopedSlot>
```

We have learned the way to handle the props in the components. The props can be validated with type checks. They can also be marked as required. We can also define default values for the component props. Apart from the props, to pass the content from parent to child, we can use the slot technique. The Slot Props can be used to pass the data back from the child to parent, which is meant to be handled in the slots itself. We can also control the content to be displayed by using the named slots too.

In the next chapter we will learn about the mixins, custom directives, plugins, and filters. We will also see how to merge the components with mixins. We will also explore the way to create new custom directives and use them.

DAY 6
Distribute Reusable Functionalities

In the previous chapter we learnt, how to move ahead with the components. We have defined the props more manageable and controlled way. Applying validation on the props in a component is very much useful in a way to control the data. Also, we saw how Slots help the components to pass the contents in between.

We will now look into the way to make the functionalities distributable. We will focus on making things more reusable in this chapter.

Mixins

As the name suggest, it gets mixed with the components. It makes reusable functionality work by mixing its content into the component.

Let's assume, we have multiple components and they share some common functionality. So in order to accommodate it, we need to merge the component with each other. So that we can only expose one component without creating repetitive code. But the there is another issue with this approach, if we merge the components into one then both components will get some extra functionalities which are not really needed for them.

To solve this kind of problem, we can take the help from Mixin. We can put those common functionalities in a mixin and use the same mixin in both the components. In this way, we don't need to merge the components.

In the below example, we will have two components with email validation in common. We will wrap that common functionality in a mixin. We will mix that mixin in both the components so that they can avail the email validation in both.

In this example, we will create a mixin called **EmailValidationMixin**. We can follow a separate folder structure for the same.

Fig 6.1: Folder structure for Mixins in a separate folder

The folder structure is not mandatory. For the shake of increase in readability and maintainability we have placed the same in a separate folder.

The mixin is a JavaScript file, which contains code for mixin.

```
export const EmailValidatorMixin = {
    methods: {
        validate_email: function(email){
            if(email == "" ){ alert("Please enter email");
            return false;}
```

```
        var mailformat = /[A-Z0-9._%+-]+@[A-Z0-9.-]+.
        [A-Z]{2,4}/igm;
         if (mailformat.test(email)){
            alert("Email is Valid");
         }
         else{
            alert("Invalid email");
         }
      }
   }
 }
```

When we mix this mixin with the components, they will get access to the **validate_email** method defined in here.

In order to use the mixin in the component, we need to import the mixin in that component and declare the mixing under the mixins tag.

```
<template>
    <div>
        <table style="border: 0px;">
            <tr>
                <td>Customer Email Address</td>
                <td><input type="text" v-model="cust_
                email" /></td>
                <td><input type="button" v-on:click='validate_
                email(cust_email)' value="Validate" /></td>
            </tr>
            <tr>
                <td>Customer Number</td>
                <td><input type="text" v-model="cust_num"
                /></td>
                <td><input type="button"
                v-on:click='validate_customer()'
                value="Validate" /></td>
            </tr>
        </table>
    </div>
</template>

<script>
    import {EmailValidatorMixin} from '../mixins/
```

```
EmailValidator.js'
export default {
    name: "CustomerValidation",
    data() {
        return{
            cust_email: "",
            cust_num: ""
        }
    },
    mixins: [EmailValidatorMixin],
    methods: {
        validate_customer: function(){
            if(this.cust_num == "" ){ alert("Please
            enter Customer Number"); return false;}
            if(this.cust_num.indexOf("CN") == -1){
                alert("Invalid Customer Number");
            }
            else{
                alert("Customer Number is Valid");
            }
        }
    }

}
</script>
```

As we can see the components can directly access the method from the mixin. In the onclick event of the button, we can get the method called directly. The similar implementation can be done for the **EmployeeValidation** component too.

```
<template>
    <div>
        <table style="border: 0px;">
            <tr>
                <td>Employee Email Address</td>
                <td><input type="text" v-model="emp_email"
                /></td>
                <td><input type="button" v-on:click='validate_
                email(emp_email)' value="Validate" /></td>
            </tr>
            <tr>
```

```
            <td>Employee Number</td>
            <td><input type="text" v-model="emp_num"
            /></td>
            <td><input type="button"
v-on:click='validate_customer()' value="Validate" /></td>
        </tr>
    </table>
  </div>
</template>

<script>
    import {EmailValidatorMixin} from '../mixins/
EmailValidator.js'
    export default {
        name: "EmployeeValidation",
        data() {
            return{
                emp_email: "",
                emp_num: ""
            }
        },
        mixins: [EmailValidatorMixin],
        methods: {
            validate_customer: function(){
                if(this.emp_num == "" ){ alert("Please
                enter Employee Number"); return false;}
                if(this.emp_num.indexOf("EM") == -1){
                    alert("Invalid Employee Number");
                }
                else{
                    alert("Employee Number is Valid");
                }
            }
        }


    }
</script>
```

Like the **CustomerValidation** component, we can also call the same
method on click of the button directly. It behaves as if the function is
defined in that same component.

Life cycle hook in Mixins

Let's consider a situation, when the life cycle hook gets implemented in the mixin. Also, the same hook implemented in the component. In this situation, Mixin wins the race. The hook defined in the mixin gets invoked first, followed by the hook in the component.

```
export const EmailValidatorMixin = {
    created: function(){
        alert("Mixin created");
    },
    methods: {
        validate_email: function(email){
            if(email == "" ){ alert("Please enter email");
            return false;}
            var mailformat = /[A-Z0-9._%+-]+@[A-Z0-9.-]+.
            [A-Z]{2,4}/igm;
            if (mailformat.test(email)){
                alert("Email is Valid");
            }
            else{
                alert("Invalid email");
            }
        }
    }
}
```

As shown in the example, we have added an alert in the created hook of the mixin. Now, let's add the same in one of our component to test it.

```
import {EmailValidatorMixin} from '../mixins/
EmailValidator.js'
export default {
    name: "CustomerValidation",
    data() {
        return{
            cust_email: "",
            cust_num: ""
        }
    },
    mixins: [EmailValidatorMixin],
    methods: {
```

```
        validate_customer: function(){
            if(this.cust_num == "" ){ alert("Please
            enter Customer Number"); return false;}
            if(this.cust_num.indexOf("CN") == -1){
                alert("Invalid Customer Number");
            }
            else{
                alert("Customer Number is Valid");
            }
        }
    },
    created: function(){
        alert("Component created");
    }

}
```

As seen in the code we have use two *alerts* to check the execution sequence. When we run it in the browser, the *alert* message in the mixin is displayed first, and then the alert in the component.

Merging in mixins

As learnt previously, mixin gets merged with the component. That also means, the data object in the mixin also gets merged with the components too.

```
export const DataMergerMixin = {
    data: function(){
        return{
            message : "Message from mixin"
        }
    }
}
```

We will define some data in the components.

```
<template>
    <div>
        {{ $data }}
    </div>
</template>

<script>
```

```
    import {DataMergerMixin} from '../mixins/
    DataMergerMixin.js'
    export default {
        name: "DataMerge",
        data() {
            return{
                component_message: "This is a component
                message",
            }
        },
        mixins: [DataMergerMixin],
    }
</script>
```

The result of {{ **$data** }} would be the combination of both data object.

```
{ "component_message": "This is a component message",
"message": "Message from mixin" }
```

Point to note here, if the data variable names would be same in both mixin and the components, then the data variable of the component will only get printed. Let's rename the **component_message** variable in the components as **message**.

```
<template>
    <div>
        {{ $data }}
    </div>
</template>

<script>
    import {DataMergerMixin} from '../mixins/
    DataMergerMixin.js'
    export default {
        name: "DataMerge",
        data() {
            return{
                message: "This is a component message",
            }
        },
        mixins: [DataMergerMixin],
    }
</script>
```

Now, both the data variable in mixin and component are same. So, the output will be overridden by the component.

```
{ "message": "This is a component message" }
```

Conflicting functions

Like conflicting data variables, in case of the conflicting functions between the component and mixin, the function in component overrides the value.

Global Mixin

Mixin defined in the global scope will be accessible to all the components. In a CLI built vue application, we can define a mixin in the **main.js**.

```
Vue.mixin({
  methods: {

    showAppInfo: function () {
    alert("Learn Vue In 7 Days")
  }
}
})
```

We have added a method named as showAppInfo, to show the application information. This should be globally accessible to all the components.

Custom Directives

We have learnt many directives in Vue having v- as a prefix. Directives like **v-model, v-if,** and so on. we have learnt are the supported directives by Vue.

Now, let's create our own custom directives. As the name suggests, the custom directives will behave in a custom way.

Creating custom directives

To create the custom directive, we need to use the Vue object. Directives will be added to the Vue object of the application.

```
Vue.directive('campaign name',
    function(el, binding, vnode) {
})
```

In the function, it accepts the following parameters to deal with the user and data.

- **el :** This stands for element. It returns the DOM object with which the directive is associated with.

- **binding :** It contains the information about the params, formatters, and so on.

- **vnode :** vnode keeps the track of the parent DOM element.

Let's create our first custom directives. We are using the Vue CLI environment to write the code. We will add the directive to **main.js** and keep accessing them.

```
Vue.directive('highlight',
    function(el, binding, vnode) {
        el.style.fontSize = '50px';
        el.style.fontWeight = 'bold';
    }
)
```

As shown in the above code, we have created a new custom directive as **highlight**. It will set the font size and the font weight of the DOM element it will get bind to.

```
<template>
    <div>
        <p v-highlight>Custom directive demo</p>
    </div>
</template>
```

The highlight directive will be used in the HTML element with a v-prefix. Here, we have added the custom directive to the **<p>** DOM element. So that the formatting will be applied to that element now.

Custom directive demo

Fig 6.2: Browser console showing custom directive added to the element

When gets rendered on screen, the directives apply the changes on the DOM element in runtime.

Passing values to custom directives

In the previous example, we have created the custom directive, which accepts no value from the external source. It sets the fixed formatting to the HTML element. We can also pass values into the custom directives. Based on those passed values, custom directives can also apply formatting.

```
Vue.directive('notify',
    function(el, binding, vnode) {
        var colour = (binding.value != undefined && binding.
        value !="") ? binding.value : "red";
        el.style.fontSize = '15px';
        el.style.fontWeight = 'bold';
        el.style.color = colour;
        el.style.backgroundColor='#ffcccc';
    }
)
```

In the code above, we have created a custom directive named as **notify**. We can pass values from outside to set the formatting of the DOM element.

In this example, we have applied the fixed formatting to the DOM element excluding the color. Then color receives the dynamic values from the user. The default color set here is, red. If no colors are available then the color of the element will be red, else the user input will be used as the color.

```
<template>
    <div>
        <p v-notify="'blue'">You have successfully landed
        in demo page</p> <br/><br/><br/>
    </div>
</template>
```

We have passed the color value from the HTML to the directive. The value needs to be passed after the "=" sign within double quotes.

Fig 6.3: Showing the screenshot of styles applied by passing the value in custom directory

In the browser, it renders with the custom color, as input by the user along with the other fixed formatting.

Arguments passing to custom directives

Like value passing, we can also pass arguments into the custom directives. To pass the arguments, we need to use : *(colon)* instead of the equal sign.

```
<template>
    <div>
        <span>Low Traffic </span>
        <div v-traffic:low  class="traffic-div"></div>
        <span>Moderate Traffic </span>
        <div v-traffic:moderate class="traffic-div"></div>
        <span>High Traffic </span>
        <div v-traffic:high class="traffic-div"></div>
    </div>
</template>

<style>
    .traffic-div{
        display: block;
        width: 85px;
        height: 85px;
        border-radius: 100%;
        margin-left: 43%;
    }
</style>
```

We have defined a dummy traffic light system with different amount of delays. Based on the arguments (Low/Moderate/High) the traffic signal will behave accordingly.

As seen in the above code, we have passed the arguments into the custom directives using : (colon). Depending upon the argument, it will change the element style to perform in the web page.

```
Vue.directive('traffic', function(el, binding, vnode){
    var intervalObj;
    var interval = 5000;
    switch(binding.arg){
      case "low":
        interval = 5000;
        break;
      case "moderate":
        interval = 10000;
        break;
      case "high":
        interval = 20000;
        break;
      case "stop":
        if(intervalObj){
          clearInterval(intervalObj);
        }
        break;
    }
    el.style.backgroundColor = 'red';
    var signalColor = ['green', 'orange', 'red'];
    var i = 0;
    intervalObj = setInterval(function(){
      if(i==3){
        i=0;
      }
      el.style.backgroundColor =  signalColor[i];
      i++;
    }, interval);

})
```

The arguments here are placed in a switch-case. Depending upon the argument passed, it will perform the task accordingly. To illustrate it, we have kept an interval of 5 seconds, 10 seconds, and 20 seconds for the low, moderate, and high respectively to change the signal color.

Low Traffic

Moderate Traffic

High Traffic

Fig 6.4: Traffic light application implementing arguments passed to custom directory

Passing Modifiers to Custom Directives

We can pass modifiers into the custom directives. Unlike the above, it will be passed using the . (dot).

```
<template>
    <div>
        <p v-markText.makeHeading.underline.
        makeCapital>Mark the text</p>
    </div>
</template>
```

In the above HTML, we have passed multiple modifiers into the custom directive **v-markText**. The formatting will be done, depending upon the order it appears.

```
Vue.directive('markText',
    function(el, binding) {
      if(binding.modifiers.underline){
          el.style.textDecoration = "underline";
      }
      if(binding.modifiers.makeCapital){
          el.style.textTransform = "uppercase";
      }
      if(binding.modifiers.makeHeading){
        el.style.fontSize = '50px';
        el.style.fontWeight = 'bold';
    }
        if(binding.modifiers.highlight){
```

```
            el.style.backgroundColor = "yellow";
        }
    }
)
```

The text gets formatted depending upon the formatters specified in the custom directive.

Hooks in custom directives

Custom directives also support hooks. This should not be confused with the vue hooks.

Following is the list of hooks (As per the Vue official documents **https://vuejs.org/v2/guide/custom-directive.html#Hook-Functions)** supported by custom directives and their descriptions.

- **bind:** Called only once, when the directive is first bound to the element. This is where you can do one-time setup work.

- **inserted:** Called when the bound element has been inserted into its parent node (this only guarantees parent node presence, not necessarily in-document).

- **update:** Called after the containing component's VNode has updated, *but possibly before its children have updated.* The directive's value may or may not have changed, but you can skip unnecessary updates by comparing the binding's current and old values (see below on hook arguments).

- **componentUpdate:** Called after the containing component's VNode and the VNodes of its children have updated.

- **unbind:** Called only once, when the directive is unbound from the element.

The most popular hooks are bind and inserted.

```
Vue.directive("custom-hook", {
  bind(el) {
      el.style.color = "red";
      console.log("Bind");
  },
  inserted(el) {
    el.style.color = "blue";
    console.log("Inserted");
  }
});
```

Since we are referring to a single element here, we can only see the color changed to **blue** only. Since the *inserted* hook gets executed after bind, the **red** color won't be visible. But certainly, we can see the sequence of the hooks executed in the console window.

Filters

Filters are the options to apply additional formatting upon the data in runtime. We can apply filters using the | (pipe) symbol in data. There are two ways we can apply filters.

Mustache interpolation:

{{ message | reverse}}

v-bind expression:

v-bind:id = record_id | format_filter

Let's create a custom filter to reverse the data. We will define the filter inside a component. We will create a new component and add this in it.

```
<template>
    <div>
        {{ message | reverse }}
    </div>
</template>

<script>
    export default {
        name: "CustomFilterDemo",
        data() {
            return{
                message: "Learn"
            }
        },
        filters: {
            reverse: function(value) {
                value = value.toString()
                var revString = ""
                for(var i=0; i<=value.length-1; i++){
                    revString = value.charAt(i) + revString
                }
```

```
            return revString
        }
    }
}
</script>
```

We have used the filters section to define the filter method.

Point to note here, in the filter function we have accepted a value parameter. But have not passed any value when we have called the same filter inside the mustache interpolation of the template. Because, it accepts the data result as the default input to the value parameter. So, whenever we have added a filter, it accepts the data as the value parameter.

In the above example, we have used the message as a data variable and added a fixed string into it as "Learn". In the reverse filter, we have reversed the message data.

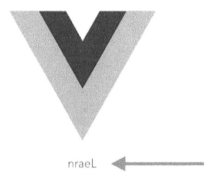

nraeL

Fig 6.6: filter applied on string

Multiple parameters in filters

We can also pass multiple parameters into a filter. In the above example, we have only one parameter as value. But we can also pass multiple parameters into a filter.

In order to see how multiple params work, we will create another filter to append a fixed string to the data value.

```
<template>
    <div>
        {{ message | append_string(" - It is actually fun." )}}
    </div>
```

```
</template>
<script>
    export default {
        name: "CustomFilterDemo",
        data() {
            return{
                message: "Learn"
            }
        },
        filters: {
            append_string: function(value, fixedString) {
                return value + fixedString
            }
        }
    }
</script>
```

In this filter function, we have two params value and fixedString. We can notice, in the template, we have only passed value for one parameter i.e the second parameter.

As stated above, the data value automatically gets set as the first parameter to the filter function. So, we need to pass the second param only.

Learn - It is actually fun.

Fig 6.7: Applying multiple params in filter on a string

Chain of filters

We can apply multiple filters to one data too. They work in sequence. That means, the data value or the result of the last filter would be the input value of the next filter.

We will use the above example to reverse the data, capitalize the reversed data and append the static string to it.

```
<template>
    <div>
        {{ message | reverse | capitalize | append_string("
- This string is reversed." )}}
    </div>
</template>

<script>
    export default {
        name: "CustomFilterDemo",
        data() {
            return{
                message: "Learn"
            }
        },
        filters: {
            capitalize: function(value){
                value = value.toString()
                var first = value.charAt(0).toUpperCase()
                var last = value.charAt(value.length-1).
                toLowerCase()
                var capValue = first + value.substring(1,
                value.length-1) + last
                return capValue
            },
            reverse: function(value) {
                value = value.toString()
                var revString = ""
                for(var i=0; i<=value.length-1; i++){
                    revString = value.charAt(i) + revString
                }
                return revString
            },
            append_string: function(value, fixedString) {
                return value + fixedString
            }

        }

    }
</script>
```

We have defined three (reverse, capitalize, and append_string) filters and used in the interpolation. As per the sequence of the filters, message is the input value of the reverse filter. The result of the reverse filter would be the input of the capitalize filter and the result of this filter would be the input of the append_string filter.

So, it first reverse the string. Then makes the reversed string capitalize. Then adds a fixed string to the reversed and capitalized string.

Nrael - This string is reversed.

Fig 6.8: *Chain of filters applied on a string*

Global filter

In the above examples, we have defined the filters inside the component. So, they can only be accessed inside the component only. We can also declare the global filters, which gets associated with the Vue object.

Let's create the same reverse filter globally to make it accessible throughout the application. We can define the same globally. If we are using Vue CLI, then **main.js** is one of the best suited places to define the same.

```
Vue.filter('reverse', function(value) {
    value = value.toString()
    var revString = ""
    for(var i=0; i<=value.length-1; i++){
        revString = value.charAt(i) + revString
    }
    return revString
})
```

As we can see in the preceding code, to make it global we need to add the filter to the Vue object.

Plugin

When you want to have some global functionality packaged together into one file and can be referenced anywhere in your project, you should definitely use a Plugin.

jQuery is a very good example of Plugin, moreover, we can easily create a Plugin with Vue. You can use all Vue concepts inside the Plugin to build it. Components, Mixins, Filters, and so on can go inside the Plugin to make it more effective and reusable for different apps.

Plugin is a good way to keep your Vue components clear and small. The biggest advantage is, you can package and share with the world or within your company for all developers to consume it in their apps.

Writing plugin is not difficult. Here is the skeleton of a plugin. It's just a JavaScript object with an install method.

```
MyPlugin.install = (Vue, options) => {
    // Plugin functionality.
}
```

This install method takes two params, Vue and options. These options are used to customize the plugin usage to fit specific needs. We will gradually see how to work with these params.

Let's start with a simple one. After creating a project through Vue CLI, add the following code inside a file, for example **myPlugin.js**.

```
export default {
    name: 'myPlugin',
    install: function (Vue, options) {
      console.log("Install started");

        // 1. add global method or property
      Vue.prototype.$myGlobalMethod = function () {
      // some logic ...
        console.log("Global Method called!");
      }
    }
  }
```

As you see, it has install function which is mandatory. When you refer this plugin in code, it would call this install function and execute everything inside it. In our example, we have declared one prototype method named as **$myGlobalMethod**, which simply logs to console.

Note: $ can be added just for naming convention for a global property/method.

To add this plugin to the project, we need to update **main.js** as follows.

```
import Vue from 'vue'
import App from './App.vue'
import MyPlugin from './plugins/myPlugin.js'

Vue.use(MyPlugin)

Vue.config.productionTip = false

new Vue({
  render: h => h(App),
}).$mount('#app')
```

The two highlighted lines are important. One tells Vue where the plugin file is. I have kept it inside the plugins folder, so the code **import MyPlugin from './plugins/myPlugin.js'** imports it from there. Next line registers the plugin for the project using the **Vue. use()** global method. These are mandatory.

Next step is to do something with the plugin. As we have a global method inside that, let's try to invoke that from a button. Quickly move to **App.vue** and add a button with a click event.

```
<template>
  <div id="app">
    <img alt="Vue logo" src="./assets/logo.png">
    <HelloWorld msg="Welcome to Your Vue.js App"/>
    <button v-on:click="invokePluginMethod">Click Me</
button>
  </div>
</template>
```

And of course, we need to define the **invokePluginMethod** something like the following:

```
export default {
  name: 'app',
  components: {
    HelloWorld
```

```
    },
    methods:{
      invokePluginMethod: function() {
        this.$myGlobalMethod()
      }
    }
}
```

The code **this.$myGlobalMethod()** actually invokes the method inside the plugin.

Now, let's run and see what happens!

Fig 6.9: Console Result for Plugin Install Started

I have opened the console at the bottom. You can see the message **Install started**. This message was added inside the install function of the myPlugin.

Next step is to click the button **Click Me**. As soon as you do that, you would see a message on console saying, **Global Method called!**. Take a loot at the following screenshot:

Fig 6.10: Console Result for Plugin Global Method Invoke

Generally, plugins are configurable. If you see the declaration, it contains a parameter in install method, which we can pass like the following as an object.

```
Vue.use(MyPlugin, { delaySeconds: 4 })
```

And this can be used to configure the plugin and do operations accordingly. Suppose, we want to delay the console log using this value. We can do like the following:

```
Vue.prototype.$myGlobalMethod = function () {
        setTimeout(() => {
            console.log("Global Method called!");
        }, options.delaySeconds * 1000);
    }
```

Here, options are the parameter to install method.

Plugins are much more than adding global methods. We can include mixins, components, directives, and so on. Let's add one directive to show a text as **Read more** and **Read less**.

So, we would add one html paragraph element with the directive to indicate how many characters we would like to show. And then after those characters, **Read more...** is shown. The paragraph would look like:

```
<p v-max-character-length="70">{{ feedbackText }}</p>
```

The directive is max-character-length which takes a value of 70. So, after 70 characters, we will show **Read more....** Let's design the directive inside the plugin.

Basically, the structure would look something like the following:

```
const ExpandSqueeze = {
    install(Vue, options) {
        Vue.directive('max-character-length', {
            bind(el, binding, vnode, oldVnode) {
                // Add logic to show "Read more..." and "Read
                less...".
            }
        })
    },
};

export default ExpandSqueeze;
```

Now inside the bind event, we need to create two anchor elements and with text as required. Also, we have underlined and added cursor as pointer. Following is the clear code:

```
const readMoreLink = document.createElement('a');
readMoreLink.innerHTML = 'Read more...';
readMoreLink.style.textDecoration = 'underline';
readMoreLink.style.cursor = 'pointer';

const readLessLink = document.createElement('a');
readLessLink.innerHTML = 'Read less...';
readLessLink.style.textDecoration = 'underline'
readLessLink.style.cursor = 'pointer';
```

Next is to attach two events to these elements so that when we click **Read more...**, it shows all text and displays **Read less...** and vice versa.

```
    readMoreLink.addEventListener('click', showAllText);
    readLessLink.addEventListener('click', showLimitedText);
```

The events would work as follows.

```
const showAllText = () => {
    el.innerHTML = `${currentHTML} `;
    el.appendChild(readLessLink);
}
const showLimitedText = () => {
    el.innerHTML = `${slicedHTML}... `;
    el.appendChild(readMoreLink);
}
```

showAllText shows all the text with **Read less...** link and **showLimitedText** shows limited text with **Read more...** link.

Putting it together would look something like the following:

```
const ExpandSqueeze = {
    install(Vue, options) {
      Vue.directive('max-character-length', {
        bind(el, binding, vnode, oldVnode) {
          const maxLimit = binding.value || 100;
          const currentHTML = el.innerHTML;
          const slicedHTML = currentHTML.slice(0,
          maxLimit);

          const readMoreLink = document.createElement('a');
          readMoreLink.innerHTML = 'Read more...';
          readMoreLink.style.textDecoration = 'underline';
```

```
      readMoreLink.style.cursor = 'pointer';

      const readLessLink = document.createElement('a');
      readLessLink.innerHTML = 'Read less...';
      readLessLink.style.textDecoration = 'underline'
      readLessLink.style.cursor = 'pointer';

      const showAllText = () => {
        el.innerHTML = `${currentHTML} `;
        el.appendChild(readLessLink);
      }

      const showLimitedText = () => {
        el.innerHTML = `${slicedHTML}... `;
        el.appendChild(readMoreLink);
      }

      readMoreLink.addEventListener('click',
      showAllText);
      readLessLink.addEventListener('click',
      showLimitedText);

      showLimitedText();
    }
  })
  },
};

  export default ExpandSqueeze;
```

At the end, **showLimitedText** is called so that we see limited text. Following screenshot proves what is said, which limits the text to 70 characters as I mentioned during the paragraph declaration.

Fig 6.11: ExpandSqueeze Plugin Output

When you click **Read more...,** it shows all the text appended with **Read less...** link.

In this chapter, we have covered how mixins helps in defining common logic and get merged with the components. We have also learnt the way to define custom directives to manage the formatting and display in the UI components. Also, we have learnt the filters and plugins.

We will learn the way to develop single page website using the state management. We will cover the state management in the next chapter.

DAY 7
Single Page Application

In the previous chapter, we discovered some ways to build reusable distributed functionalities for our Vue applications.

Routing and State Management play an important role while designing Single Page Applications (SPA). In this chapter, we will look into ways to implement these concepts in our Vue app.

HTML5 History mode would help us creating routes for SPAs that creates an easy path way for the user to go back and forth between pages dynamically without page load.

We will learn few principles with proper illustrations for State Management in Vue apps. Parent Child component interaction using props and custom events followed by state management techniques with EventBus and Global Store is what we are going to explore.

Last, but not the least, the Vuex library, which is a robust way to manage the application state will take your attention to the next level of app development with Vue.

Of course, we will take a brief look at the differences between these state management techniques to decide which one to go for.

Following are the topics we will cover:

- Creating a route
- Using the routes
- Basics of how state management works
- State management implementation using EventBus, Global Store and Vuex

What is a Route

Routng is a technique by which the requests coming to your website or webservices are guided through to the destination meaning the code which would handle them. Suppose you type **http://www.example.com/about** on the browser url box, which should point to your About.html or something else. Defining that particular rule is called Routing.

In a Single Page Apllication (SPA), Routing is the key as you really don't want your page to reload for another request. Tradional applications behave in such a way that when you click on a hyperlink, it would go to server and come with a html page. However, in SPA, the page loads one time and when you request for something by your actions on the page (like clicking a lin or button), it dynamically changes the content as per the request to load new content/page.

We will see how we can configure Routes easily with Vue for SPA. But before that, let's first understand the Routing concept and how to build routes.

Creating a Route

As Vue is component based, let's first design few components for different pages like Home, About and Contact.

Home.vue

```
<template>
  <div class="home">
    <h2>This is Home Page!</h2>
  </div>
</template>

<script>
```

```
export default {
  name: 'Home'
}
</script>
```

Contact.vue

```
<template>
  <div class="contact">
    <h2>This is Contact Page!</h2>
  </div>
</template>

<script>
export default {
  name: 'Contact'
}
</script>
```

About.vue

```
<template>
  <div class="about">
    <h2>This is About Page!</h2>
  </div>
</template>

<script>
export default {
  name: 'About'
}
</script>
```

Now we need to build a mechanism to tie up all these together to a method so that we can access the pages as urls like **www.example.com/home, www.example.com/about, www.example.com/contact.**

For that, let's define a route object for all the pages.

```
import Home from "./Home";
import About from "./About";
import Contact from "./Contact";

const routes = {
  "/": Home,
```

```
  "/home": Home,
  "/about": About,
  "/contact": Contact
};
```

Simple, isn't it! Basically, we are asking to map the routes to their respective pages. Notice that we have assigned / and /home to Home.vue as it is obvious.

However, this is not all. We still have not done anything with the routes object. If you think logically, when a request comes for a particular page say /about, we have to somehow load About.vue. Below is the code for that where we are fetching window.location. pathname and using that to retrieve the component name from the routes object.

```
export default {
  data() {
    return { current: window.location.pathname };
  },
  computed: {
    routedComponent() {
      return routes[this.current];
    }
  }
};
```

After this, we need to have a template which would load the component we retrieved. To do that, let's add the following code using :is directive with the computed data routedComponent.

```
<template>
  <component :is="routedComponent"></component>
</template>
```

Now, putting it all together we can save all these code in another component called AppRouter.vue.

```
<template>
  <component :is="routedComponent"></component>
</template>

<script>
import Home from "./Home";
import About from "./About";
import Contact from "./Contact";
```

```
const routes = {
  "/": Home,
  "/home": Home,
  "/about": About,
  "/contact": Contact
};
export default {
  data() {
    return { current: window.location.pathname };
  },
  computed: {
    routedComponent() {
      return routes[this.current];
    }
  }
};
</script>
```

Using the Routes

Everything is ready except the App.vue which would give life to this AppRouter component. Add the following code inside App.vue.

```
import AppRouter from "./components/AppRouter.vue";
```

```
export default {
  components: {
    AppRouter
  }
};
```

NOTE: App.vue is present inside root folder, but all other components discussed above are placed inside the "components" folder.

Let's run the app by npm run serve command and see if this works.

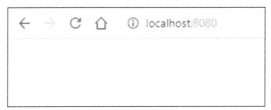

Fig7.1: Routing Initial Run No Output

Interesting! No output. That is obvious because we have not yet included the AppRouter component inside App.vue.

```
<template>
  <div>
    <app-router></app-router>
  </div>
</template>
```

Now run it again, it would display the following output!

Fig7.2: Simple Routing Example

Here we can see four outputs shown in the picture side by side. Have a close look on the Urls. Localhost:8080 and localhost:8080/home loads the same page Home.vue. That is what we wanted as declared in the routes object. About and Contact components are also loaded for localhost:8080/about and localhost:8080/contact respectively.

On a fully featured production app, however, the pages are linked to eachother. Meaning, links are present to navigate from one page to another. Something like below:

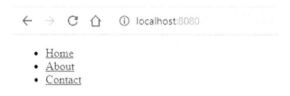

Fig7.3: Routing with Navigation Links

For this, we can add one unordered list with the routes inside App. vue.

```
<template>
  <div>
    <ul>
      <li><a href="#" @click="loadPage('/home')">Home</
a></li>
      <li><a href="#" @click="loadPage('/about')">About</
a></li>
      <li><a href="#" @click="loadPage('/
contact')">Contact</a></li>
    </ul>
    <app-router></app-router>
  </div>
</template>
```

Here loadPage is a method which would load the route into window. location.

```
export default {
  components: {
    AppRouter
  },
  methods: {
    loadPage(route) {
      window.location = route;
    }
  }
};
```

With this code in place, we can see the above output with links on each page, which loads the particular component as requested on the url passed.

Whatever we discussed so far works for normal loading of pages, that means when you click the link, the page reloads and content changes. However, in case of SPA, the page dynamically loads the contents without reloading. That is what we will learn in the next content.

Routing in SPA

With some more changes to the code above, we can acheive routing for one SPA app. Basically, the page should not reload. HTML5 History Mode would help us manage the history of pages. Let's get started.

The History API has different methods which we can use. The pushState method would replace the window.location and does not perform a reload.

Let's update the App.vue to implement pushState method.

```
loadPage(route) {
  //window.location = route;
  history.pushState(null, null, route)
}
```

Let's not focus on the first two parameters for now. Third parameter is for the route, which we passed.

The next step is to react to the route changes. If you remember, AppRouter component helps us to render the actual page. That means routedComponent computed property should be updated, which implies an update to this.current variable. We will see how that is done in a while.

But before that, let's modularize the history related operations. Name it as history.js.

First add the push method.

```
export const push = route => {
    window.history.pushState(null, null, route);
  }
}
```

History would also listen to changes in the route, for that, we need to implement a method called listen that stores the callback methods in a listeners array.

```
const listeners = [];

export const push = route => {
  window.history.pushState(null, null, route);
};

export const listen = fn => {
  listeners.push(fn);
};
```

Now the push method should take the responsibility to notify by iterating the listeners and call the callback functions passing the route as a parameter.

```
export const push = route => {
    const previousRoute = window.location.pathname;
    window.history.pushState(null, null, route);
    listeners.forEach(listener => listener(route,
    previousRoute));
};
```

As we are done wih the history module, let's start using that inside the App.vue.

```
import AppRouter from "./components/AppRouter.vue";
import { push } from "./history";
export default {
  components: {
    AppRouter
  },
  methods: {
    loadPage(route) {
      //window.location = route;
      //history.pushState(null, null, route)
      push(route);
    }
  }
};
```

Instead of using history.pushState method, now we are using calling push method directly which is residing inside history.js.

We have more work to do. The AppRouter component should know about the change in the route when we navigate between pages. And that is because there is a this.current variable which stores the current route.

```
// Other codes here...
import { listen } from "../history";

export default {
  created() {
    listen((route, previousRoute) => {
        this.current = route
      });
  },
  // More codes...
};
```

The listen method is called inside created hook because we need to set the listener mechanism once. That is because everything else automatically works next time when you call push for subsequent requests. If you see the push method inside the AppRouter, that actually calls the mthod registered into the listener array.

Now, if you run the app, it will change the route and page content on button clicks. However, if you click on browser back and forward buttons, it won't work.

To complete the SPA routing, we need to add another small chunk of code inside AppRouter and the complete code looks like below:

```
export default {
  created() {
    listen((route, previousRoute) => {
      debugger;
        this.current = route
      });
    window.addEventListener(
      "popstate",
      event => (this.current = window.location.pathname)
    );
  },
  data() {
    return { current: window.location.pathname };
  },
  computed: {
    routedComponent() {
      return routes[this.current];
    }
  }
};
```

So, the popstate method is called wheen we click back and forward button of browser, thereby setting up the thei.current value.

Thus, we completed the SPA routing with Vue. You can find the codes in Github. Try it and see that you can see the page contents dynamically without page load, when you click on the buttons on the page or browser back and forward buttons.

State Management

Components are the building blocks of Vue application. It's important how the application shows us updated data evertime a change occurs. That means the data update should ensure integrity among the components.

Let's go through a step by step example to understand how we can manage state for the data in a vue js app.

Array Component Example

One example ArrayComponent might look like the following.

```
<template>
  <div>
    <h2>The numbers are {{ numberArray }}!</h2>
  </div>
</template>

<script>
export default {
  name: 'ArrayComponent',
  data () {
    return {
      numberArray: [3, 8, 0, 9]
    }
  },
}
</script>
```

The data function is responsible to make the Vue app reactive. So, any change to the data property will trigger a rerender of the view if the property is being used.

Now let's go another step and try to manipulate this array from another component. Basically, we are trying to access or update this property from other components while asking all components to take the fresh data. When you start to operate on data properties which are reactive in nature from different components, the state of the data becomes very very important. That is where our topic of discussion comes into picture.

These data properties when shared across multiple components can be called component level data or application level data.

Parent to Child Component data passing using Props

To start with, let's try to pass data from one component to other using props.

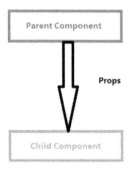

Fig7.4: Pictorial representation of Parent to Child Communication using Props

A parent component can be like:

```
<template>
  <div>
    <ChildComponent :numberArray="numberArray" />
  </div>
</template>

<script>
import    ChildComponent from "./ChildComponent";
export default {
  name: "ParentComponent",
  data() {
    return {
      numberArray: [100, 677, 987]
    };
  },
  components: {
    ChildComponent
  }
};
</script>
```

The important thing to notice here is <ChildComponent :numberArray="numberArray" /> by which we are trying to pass the data to the ChildComponent. Let's see the code of ChildComponent.

```
<template>
  <div>
    <h2>The numbers are {{ numberArray }}!</h2>
  </div>
</template>

<script>
export default {
  name: "ChildComponent",
  props: {
    numberArray: Array
  }
};
</script>
```

To catch the property, we declared that as an Array in ChildComponent and rendered it inside a template. Output is shown below.

Fig7.5: Output of Parent to Child Communication using Props

Child to Parent Component data update using Custom Events

Now that we did this, let's try to go in the opposite way. From Child to Parent. Props can't be used here as that is uni-directional approach. Vue Custom Events comes to our rescue where we can notify the Parent about a change to the array.

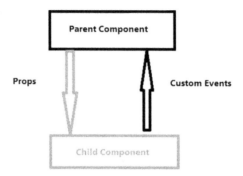

Fig7.6: *Pictorial representation of Parent and Child Communication using Props and Custom Events*

Adding a number to the array from Child is something which we can try quickly.

```
<h2>The numbers are {{ numberArray }}!</h2>
<input v-model="number" type="number" />
<button @click="$emit('add-number', Number(number))">
    Add new number
</button>
```

There is a textbox which binds the captured input to number data property.

Notice the button which has a click event that emits add-number custom event with the captured number value (converted to number using Number()) from the textbox above it. We need to have a listener for this custom event on Parent so that we can add the number entered into the numberArray.

```
<ChildComponent :numberArray="numberArray" @add-
number="numberArray.push($event)" />
```

You can see the listener pushes the number into the array. Refer the screenshot below.

The numbers are [100, 677, 987, 78]!

Fig7.7: *Output of Parent and Child Communication using Props and Custom Events*

Thus, we completed exploring two techniques to communicate between Parent Child using property and custom events. But how to communicate between two child components? That is the next thing we will learn.

When we say communication between two child components, that means we are talking about two isolated components with absolutely no dependency on each other. While using custom events, one component became parent as it rendered another component as a child. That is the mandatory condition with custom events. Therefore, in the case of isolated components, we can't use custom events.

There are few methods which we can use to manage state between independent components.

- EventBus
- Global Store
- Vuex

EventBus

EventBus helps to implement a publish and subscribe pattern. By the help of EventBus, we can easily work with custom event communication between components. Although we learnt that independent components can't communicate through custom events, however, EventBus is something global in nature which manages the communication. Let's get started.

Add a js file named as event-bus.js with the following code to instantiate.

```
import Vue from 'vue';
export const EventBus = new Vue();
```

Now we need to add two new isolated components, one which can add numbers to the array and the other which would display the results.

AddNumber.vue would look like below:

```
<template>
  <div>
    <input v-model="number" type="number" />
    <button @click="addNumber">
    Add new number
```

```
    </button>
  </div>
</template>

<script>
import { EventBus } from "../event-bus.js";
export default {
  name: "AddNumber",
  data() {
    return {
      number: 0
    };
  },
  methods: {
    addNumber() {
      EventBus.$emit("add-number", Number(this.number));
    }
  }
};
</script>
```

Basically we have added a method addNumber() which emits the add-number event using the EventBus instance with data number which is bound with the textbox.

Now it's just a matter of listening to the add-number event emitted by EventBus. Let's add the component which would show us the numbers.

```
<template>
  <div>
    <h2>{{ numbers }}</h2>
  </div>
</template>

<script>
import { EventBus } from "../event-bus.js";
export default {
  name: "ShowNumbers",
  data() {
    return {
      numbers: [900, 200, 300]
    };
```

```
  },
  created() {
    EventBus.$on("add-number", number => {
      this.numbers.push(number);
    });
  }
};
</script>
```

Notice the EventBus listener event EventBus.$on("add-number", number => {...}); that is responsible to listen to the emitted event for adding a number.

When you include both these AddNumber.vue and ShowNumbers. vue in App.vue and implement them inside template, it would look like below:

```
<template>
  <div id="app">
    <add-number></add-number>
    <show-numbers></show-numbers>
  </div>
</template>
```

So, the basic operation can be shown in the following diagram.

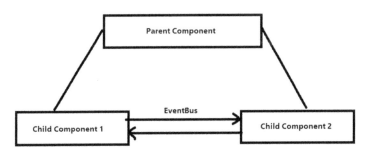

Fig7.8: Pictorial representation of Child to Child Communication using EventBus

Now run the app and see it working on browser.

Fig7.9: Output of Child Components Interaction through EventBus

According to our example, EventBus seems very easy to setup and implement in the app. However, it comes with disadvantages which can't be ignored in a prod ready application with a lot of components.

The reason, it will fail to meet the expectations is due to the emission of events through EventBus. As the app grows and more components are added, it becomes difficult to keep track of the events emitted and thus, maintenance is a pain in this technique.

Global Store

It's something very common and obvious pattern to handle application data. Technique involves creating a store which stores the data required including the methods to manage the state of the application.

Let's add one store named as store.js.

```
export const store = {
    state: {
      numberArray: [500, 250, 390]
    },
    addNumber(newNumber) {
      this.state.numberArray.push(newNumber);
    }
};
```

The store contains the numberArray inside the state object and addNumber method which pushes a new number to the state. numberArray. Now we need to use this store in our components where we would add and show the array.

StoreAddNumber.vue

```
<template>
  <div>
    <input v-model="number" type="number" />
    <button @click="addNumber(number)">
     Add new number
    </button>
  </div>
</template>

<script>
import { store } from "../store.js";

export default {
  name: "StoreAddNumber",
  data() {
    return {
      number: 0
    };
  },
  methods: {
    addNumber(number) {
      store.addNumber(Number(number));
    }
  }
};
</script>
```

Simple, isn't it. We refered the store.js inside this component and inside addNumber method we are calling the associated method using the store object.

Likewise let's add the display method.

```
<template>
  <div>
    <h2>{{ storeState.numberArray }}</h2>
  </div>
</template>

<script>
import { store } from "../store.js";

export default {
```

```
  name: "StoreNumbersDisplay",
  data() {
    return {
      storeState: store.state
    };
  }
};
</script>
```

We are just displaying the numberArray from the store object. Works like a charm due to the reactivity nature of Vue! When numberArray is updated, it is automatically getting reflected on the other components using that. Here is the output.

Fig7.10: *Output of Independent Component Interaction through Global Store*

Here is the pictorial representation.

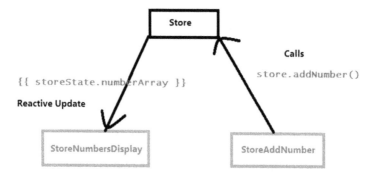

Fig7.11: *Pictorial representation of Independent Component Interaction through Global Store*

Few things to note here before we move forward.

AddNumber: directly updates the data by invoking store method. This can be tagged as *Store Action*.

Method inside Store: changes the state of the data, which can be defined as *Store Mutation*.

ShowNumbers: just gets the store data and displays, which can denoted as a *Store Getter*.

Thus, the whole flow can be described as an *Action* triggers a *Mutation*. Then Mutation mutates the state of data which then affects the View and Components because *Getters* are used to retrieve the data from Store.

The reason we discussed the above is because we are going to use them in the next section.

Vuex

Whatever we discussed above resembles Flux like architecture to manage the state. Vuex is actually a Flux-like state management library used for State Management.

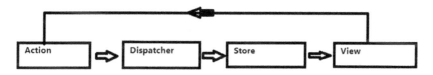

Fig7.12: Pictorial representation of Vuex

Note: Facebook introduced Flux, which is actually a design pattern. This design pattern supports one-way data pipeline between four parts named as Action, Dispatcher, Store and View. Pictorial representation would look like below:

Let's start by creating the store (store.js) using Vuex.

```
export default new Vuex.Store({
    state,
    mutations,
    actions,
    getters
});
```

If you remember the important points in the last section, Vuex uses the similar structure. Let's define one by one.

The **State** is nothing but the conttainer of data which will be shared within the application.

```
const state = {
    numberArray: [9090, 2090, 3087]
};
```

Next is **Mutations**, which are responsible to directly mutate the state of the store.

```
const mutations = {
    ADD_NUMBER(state, payload) {
      state.numberArray.push(payload);
    }
};
```

Mutations can have access to the state by the first argument. The argument payload is optional.

NOTE: The naming convention of mutations follow the rule of capital letters so that it can be distinguished from other methods across the app.

Now **Actions**, which exists to invoke these mutations.

```
const actions = {
    addNumber(context, number) {
      context.commit("ADD_NUMBER", number);
    }
};
```

Here context object provides us the power to access other properties of store like state and getters. This can play an important role for business logic inside the Actions. The commit function here helps to invoke associated mutation with payload as "number".

Last but not the least, the **Getters**, which help us to retreive the data from state.

```
const getters = {
    getNumbers(state) {
      return state.numberArray;
    }
};
```

To use all these Vuex features, we have to write few lines at the top.

```
import Vue from "vue";
import Vuex from "vuex";

Vue.use(Vuex);
```

However, this won't work because we don't have this package in our app. For that, run this command.

```
npm install vuex -save
```

Putting it all together, the store.js will look the below:

```
import Vue from "vue";
import Vuex from "vuex";

Vue.use(Vuex);

const state = {
    numberArray: [9090, 2090, 3087]
};

const mutations = {
    ADD_NUMBER(state, payload) {
      state.numberArray.push(payload);
    }
};

const actions = {
    addNumber(context, number) {
      context.commit("ADD_NUMBER", number);
    }
};

const getters = {
    getNumbers(state) {
      return state.numberArray;
    }
};

export default new Vuex.Store({
    state,
    mutations,
    actions,
    getters
});
```

The store is done, but that last step is to tell Vue that we have a store. Update your main.js code to include store in Vue object declaration.

```
new Vue({
  render: h => h(App),
  store
}).$mount('#app')
```

To consume the store, we can add components which can read or mutate data. In a component you can have a simple computed property to read the data from store with the help of getters.

```
getNumbers() {
    return this.$store.getters.getNumbers;
  }
```

The component as a whole would look like:

```
<template>
  <div>
    <h2>{{ getNumbers }}</h2>
  </div>
</template>

<script>
export default {
  name: "ShowNumbers",
  computed: {
    getNumbers() {
      return this.$store.getters.getNumbers;
    }
  }
};
</script>
```

Let me show you the method which can be added to any component, which can mutate the data in store.

```
methods: {
    addNumber(number) {
      this.$store.dispatch("addNumber", Number(number));
    }
  }
```

This method can be invoked on button click to add a number to the array using $store.dispatch. Let's have a quick look at the output on browser.

Fig7.13: Output of State Manageement with Vuex

Advantages

Vuex provides us simple interface to deal with state of data in our application. State management becomes easy with Actions, Mutations, Getters.

Let me show you another cool feature which is integrated with Vue js dev tools for Vuex. You can actually keep track of mutations in it. See the screenshot below.

Fig7.14: Vuex inside Vue Dev Tools

When you click on "Add new Number", it adds the data to the array and displays including a ADD_NUMBER row inside the Dev Tool. It can show you the payload and mutation type as well that is shown as 1212 and ADD_NUMBER respectively.

What's interesting is that it shows you all the data inside state and getters for reference. Moreover, it also has option to revert this mutation and take the state back to the previous by clicking one icon on the mutation row. Let me show you that icon below.

Fig7.15: Reverting a Mutation from Vuex Tab of Vue Dev Tools

There is one option to time travel to different state when you have more than one mutations registered on the dev tool. Another icon on the mutation row itself. When you click that icon, it would change the state on the fly. Let it be a home work for you. Let us know if you don't find it.

Analysis of Different State Management Techniques

We discovered all the techniques to manage the state of application data. However, you can select any of these according to your requirements by analysing the pros and cons.

EventBus

EventBus is very easy to set up and work, but comes with the disadvantage of no such possible way to keep track of the changes. As application grows with more components, it becomes difficult to know who is consuming the Bus to do what.

Global Store

It is something centralized and easy to understand as well as implement. However, the concept does not have explicit definitions to for the store and state changes.

Vuex

The most efficient way to manage state in Vue application. Also has integration with Vue dev tools. However, you need a little bit of understanding of Flux architecture.

Remember that Vuex is not the only library who can manage state in Vue apps. There are other libraries who can do the job like redux-vue **(https://github.com/nadimtuhin/redux-vue)** and vuejs-redux **(https://github.com/titouancreach/vuejs-redux)**.

In this chapter, we learnt few important advance concepts of Vue. Routes in Vue play an important role for loading the pages dynamically as we use it for Single Page Applications. We understood the concept of Routing and how to implement in a SPA.

Different State Management principles is what we learnt next with appropriate examples. Data transfer between parent and child components can be done using props and custom events. However, when it comes to communicate between isolated components with zero coupling, then EventBus, Global Store and Vuex come into the picture.

EventBus provides us an convinient way to implement publish and subscribe pattern for the custom events so that components can emit events which can be listened by any component with the help of EventBus object.

Global Store is just an object which stores the data as well as the event responsible to update the data. The components can refer to this store object to either get the data ot update the data, thus managing the state.

The most efficient way we discovered was Vuex which provides us well defined structure to build the store for Mutation, Actions and Getters. Vue dev tools has an inbuilt integration with Vuex for keeping track of the mutations.

In the next chapter, we will talk about server side rendering, but most importantly, we will find differences with other frameworks in the market that would not only help you to compare the features but also guide you towards what best suits for you and your career.

Appendix

With Day-7 we have concluded the VueJS learning. We have travelled all the way from normal view page designing with Vuejs to the components design. We also learnt the way to create components, making them reusable, adding more feature and formats to them using the mixins, filters, and so on. Also, we have covered the routing and state management, which will help the readers as a steppingstone towards the Vuejs app development.

In this topic, we will discuss the alternatives and possibilities using VueJs. None of the items would be cover in detail. Reader can choose to skip this topic.

We will showcase an alternate way of template designing by using the render functions and JSX. At the end, we will see a quick comparison view of the frameworks with Vuejs.

Render functions

In our previous chapters, we have learnt how we can design the templates for the components. The templates are mostly written in HTML syntaxes. These template designs are enough to develop most of the application that we use.

But there are in certain cases, when we need to use the *render functions*. They are useful mostly in writing dynamic component addition use cases. In those situations, they are useful to manage the effective use of resources.

How does it different than the template

Unlike the templates written in HTML, it is mostly the Javascript. We need to add the HTML elements into the DOM using Javascript. We use the **render** hook to define and render the HTML elements using Javascript.

Element gets created using the **createElement** function of Javascript.

Let's define a template

Let's define a template using the render method. We will create a simple span to display the text on screen.

```
<script>
export default {
  name: 'Hello World',
  render(createElement) {
    let topElement = createElement('div',[
      createElement('p', [
        createElement('span', 'Hello world'),
        ])
    ])
    return topElement
  }
}
</script>
```

In this example, we have used the **createElement** method to create element in DOM. It accepts the elements in the tree structure. As it can be seen, we have defined a **<div/>** as the parent element. Inside the **<div/>**, we have placed a **<p/>** tag and then a **<span/>** inside that. The text goes inside the **<span/>**. On render, it will render the elements accordingly.

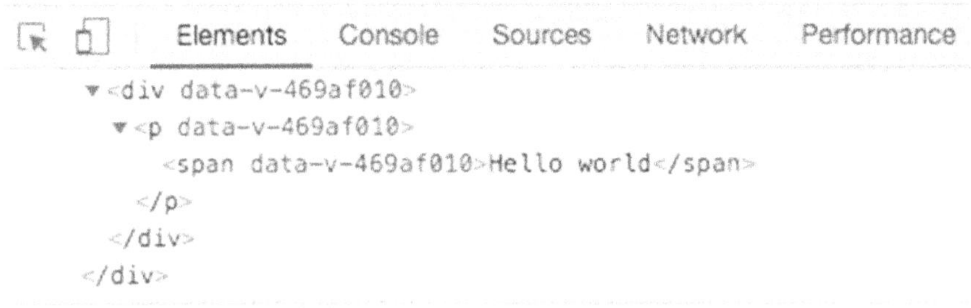

Elements   Console   Sources   Network   Performance

```
▼<div data-v-469af010>
  ▼<p data-v-469af010>
      <span data-v-469af010>Hello world</span>
    </p>
  </div>
</div>
```

Fig 8.1: HTML view of the component after rendering

Arguments of createElement method

It accepts the following arguments:

```
// @returns {VNode}
createElement(
  // {String | Object | Function}
  // An HTML tag name, component options, or async
  // function resolving to one of these. Required.
  'div',

  // {Object}
  // A data object corresponding to the attributes
  // you would use in a template. Optional.
  {
    // (see details in the next section below)
  },

  // {String | Array}
  // Children VNodes, built using 'createElement()',
  // or using strings to get 'text VNodes'. Optional.
  [
    'Some text comes first.',
    createElement('h1', 'A headline'),
    createElement(MyComponent, {
      props: {
        someProp: 'foobar'
      }
    })
  ]
)
```

Image source : https://vuejs.org/v2/guide/

Fig 8.2: Argument accepted by createElement method

Adding multiple elements

We can add multiple elements by using the **createElement** method. We will keep expanding the above example by adding the elements into it.

```
<script>
export default {
  name: 'Hello World',
  render(createElement) {
    let topElement = createElement('div',[
      createElement('p', [
        createElement('span', 'Hello world'),
        createElement('br'),
        createElement('span',{ style: { color: 'red',
        fontSize: '24px' }}, 'Hello vuejs'),
        createElement('br'),
        createElement('a',{ style: { color: 'blue',
        fontSize: '24px' }, attrs: {href: 'http://
        examplelink.com'}}, 'Hello Learner'),
        createElement('br'),
        createElement('span',{ style: { color: 'green',
        fontSize: '54px', fontFamily: 'cursive' }}, this.
        msg),
        createElement('br'),
        createElement('span',{ style: { color: 'green',
        fontSize: '34px', fontFamily: 'cursive' }},
        this.$slots.default)
        ])
    ])
    return topElement

  },
  props: {
    msg: String
  }
}
</script>
```

In the **<span>** containing the **Hello vuejs** text, we have added the styles in it. It takes the arguments using **style** tag. Also, we can notice in the **<a>** tag, we have defined the HTML attributes such as **href** under the **attrs** tag. We can also notice that prop of the component can also be added to the element using a span.

To render the slot, we have used **this.$slots.default** to get the slot value and place that inside the span tag.

Similarly, we can also add css classes, component properties, events, directives, slots, and so on to the elements using the class, props, on, directives, slots tags, and so on respectively.

Hello world

Hello vuejs

Hello Learner

Welcome to Your Vue.js App

Test the slot

Fig 8.3: UI using render function

Here is the output which shows the output of the tree structured createElement method.

JSX

It is actually a short form standing for Javascript Expressions. This approach of writing code in Javascript and XML styled representation, invented by the FaceBook engineering team. This approach is mostly used in ReactJS. Vue also supports JSX. We can use it to create the component templates.

It is more readable and maintainable than the render functions. These would the XML tag-like writing inside the Javascript functions.

Note: To compile the vue JSX code, we need to add the babel plugin to use JSX with vue.

Component using JSX

We will create a sample component using JSX to display a simple message on screen.

```
<script>
export default {
  name: 'Hello JSX',
  render(h) {
    return (
      <div>
        <p>
          <h1> Hello from JSX</h1>
        </p>
      </div>
    )
  }
}
</script>
```

As we can see in the above code snippet, we have used the same render function to create the templates. The tags are added and returned to the view from the render function.

Aliasing `createElement` to `h` is a common convention you'll see in the Vue ecosystem and is actually required for JSX. Starting with version 3.4.0 of the Babel plugin for Vue, we automatically inject `const h = this.$createElement` in any method and getter (not functions or arrow functions), declared in ES2015 syntax that has JSX, so you can drop the `(h)` parameter. With prior versions of the plugin, your app would throw an error if `h` was not available in the scope.

Image source : https://vuejs.org/v2/guide/

Fig 8.4: As per the official document, createElement replaced with h

It will normally display the string on screen.

Hello from JSX

Fig 8.5: *Rendered HTML using JSX*

In the console window, we can mark the hierarchy of the elements and the string as defined in the script.

Display the props

As a component, we can have props defined in it. The props are the ones which gets the values from the parent. If we look into the code snippet, we can mark the text display format difference. Here instead of the mustache representation, we are using the {} (single curly braces) to render the text on screen.

```
<script>
export default {
  name: 'Hello JSX',
  render() {
    return (
      <div>
        <p> {this.msg} </p>
      </div>
    )
  },
  props: {
    msg: String
  }
}
</script>
```

Let's extend the current example and add components into it. Here, we will import the component that we have already created in this chapter.

```
<script>
import HelloWorld from './HelloWorld.vue'
export default {
  name: 'Hello JSX',
  components: {
    HelloWorld
  },
  render() {
    return (
      <div>
        <p>
          <h1> Hello from JSX</h1>
        </p>
        <p> {this.msg} </p>
        <HelloWorld msg="This is hello world component"></
HelloWorld>
      </div>
    )
  },
  props: {
    msg: String
  }
}
</script>
```

We have imported the **HelloWorld** component here and added that to the page.

Fig 8.6: *Render component UI using JSX*

We can use with slots, formatters, and many more, which is beyond the scope of this topic. We have covered, how to use JSX and how it works with Vue.

Comparing Vue

Vue is a progressive Javascript framework built on top of Javascript. It uses virtual DOM to update the elements and render them on the browser. Like Vue, there are several other pretty similar frameworks present. They can also work like vue. Many times, we need to decide while choosing a framework for an application development. So, to choose we need to compare between them. We will compare with some popular frameworks with vue.

React vs Vue

React is also one of the most popular Javascript framework being used for application development. Like vue, it also uses virtual DOM to update and render the elements in the browser. React also has the component based development capability similar to Vue.

Component template designing

React	Vue
It uses JSX compulsorily to design the template. We need to learn the JSX styled way of writing.	It uses HTML, CSS along with Javascript to design the template. Also supports JSX and render functions to design the template too.
Since JSX in the way to write XML styled code in Javascript, developer can utilize the full power of Javascript to work with.	Since HTML and CSS are mostly the basic needed skills for the web development, it is easy to learn and adopt.
Mostly, it is designed for large scale applications. So, to include React into the projects, a way ahead planning is required from the beginning of the project. Using React in small applications would be an overkilling effort.	It is a lightweight framework that can be included easily in the project. So, it can be included in both small and large scale applications. Even it can also be added to ongoing applications easily with minimum effort.

Component tree rendering

React	Vue
React uses the nested component development approach. So that the components arranged in a parent child relationship.	Like React, it also uses nested component development approach and placed the components in a child parent architecture.
On state change, it renders the whole components sub tree. In order to avoid the whole sub tree rendering, we can also follow the implementation of life hooks like **shouldComponentUpdate**, and so on.	It keeps track of each component. So, incase of any changes in prop/data, it automatically identifies the component and update the relevant ones. So basically, the rendering performance is handled by Vue.

CSS file structured

React	Vue
In the react project, we can see separate CSS files for components as it follows the component specific CSS file approach. This approach keeps the design files separate from the component file.	If we create our project using Vue CLI we can notice no, CSS files by default included. Infact the CSS placed in the same component file under the **<style>** tag. It follows singe file design approach.
But there is no restriction in customizing the CSS file structures differently as per need.	Like React, CSS file structures can also be customized differently as per need.

Data mutation

React	Vue
React uses state to mutate data on screen. It won't allow a direct modification of the data. We need to set the state variable in order to make the mutation in effect.	Unlike React, Vue uses objects to mutate data. On updating the object, Vue assumes the state change and reflect the same in the DOM.
We need to use **setState** to update. For example, if we want to change the country from US to India. Then we need to do the following, **this.setState({ country: "India" })**	We can consider the same example to change the country from US to India. Vue follows the following approach to set the object. **this.country = "India"**

There is more difference in the syntaxes and semantics of both the frameworks. The handing of variables, handling of events, dealing with child/parent components, and so on. differs between React and Vue. But they are mostly on the coding syntaxes, which we cannot cover all. We have covered most basic conceptual differences above.

Angular vs Vue

The formerly and popularly known Angular 2 (current version is 6, which writing of this book) is being referred as Angular here. It is completely different than the AngularJS. We will compare Angular here with Vue.

Learning curve

Angular	Vue
Angular uses TypeScript to write the code. The static type checking in TypeScript can be very helpful in case of large applications.	Vue uses the plain Javascript with HTML to work for the application. Vue can also be included in the small scale apps as well.
It is more complex for the developers, who are trying to use it without TypeScript.	It loosely supports the TypeScript with some formatters and typings. They are still in improving state.
Developers need to learn the TypeScript and syntaxes in order to work with it.	Since it uses plain JS, and HTML, the learning curve is steeper.

Performance

Performance wise both Angular and Vue looks very much similar. Angular uses mostly Ahead of Time compilation to product the end output size considerably small. However, Vue also produces smaller sizes too.

Conceptual differences

Angular	Vue
Directives in Angular, mostly resembles with components in Vue. They contain everything and are considered as more powerful.	Directives are not so feature rich like Angular.
Filters works the same way as Vue.	Filters works same way as Angular. Additionally, they have read/write options.

Javascript frameworks are not limited to only to the above. We have only made a comparison between the popular frameworks. Since the above comparison is mostly developer centric, it would help the developers to take mostly the correct decision to choose one technology over the other while starting up with any project.

In this chapter, we have covered the alternative ways to design the Vue template. We have only covered a basic part of it. We also saw a comparison of couple of frameworks with VueJs.

When we say, we are ending up with this learning, we mean, the reader must have an idea of how Vue works as an framework. Starting from the life cycle hook to components, would give a fare idea of VueJS framework to work with it. We have also learnt a very useful way of creating reusable elements such as components, plugins, filters, directives, and so on. The state management example will also help the developer to visualize the application design way.

Certainly, it is not possible to cover everything and every knowledge about a framework in a single book. This book would be quick reference for the developers while working in the real environment.

www.ingramcontent.com/pod-product-compliance
Lightning Source LLC
LaVergne TN
LVHW022342060326
832902LV00022B/4191